"No No...

A Celebra...
in Nor...

"No Nobler County"

A Celebration of Climbing in Northumberland

Edited by
Martin Cooper

Published by
The Northumbrian Mountaineering Club, 1995

© Northumbrian Mountaineering Club

ISBN: 0 0504686 22

British Library Cataloguing in Publication Data.
A catalogue record for this book is available from the British Library.

Front cover:
Gates of Eden, Ravensheugh Crag. Climber: Mike Arnold.
Photograph: Any Birtwistle.

Frontispiece:
Angus McDonald climbing at Crag Lough, 1945.

Back cover:
Dressed for the occasion: John Earl and Bob Hutchinson
after the first ascent of The Butcher, Jack Rock, in 1973.
Photograph: John Earl collection.

CONTENTS

Introduction	1
Thanks, It's a Privilege *Bob Bell*	4
The Northumbrian Mountaineering Club, 1945 – 1995	7
Presidents of the Club, 1945 – 1995	8
The Formation of the NMC and Its Early Years *Martin Cooper and Angus MacDonald*	10
Great Gable, Christmas Eve 1944 *Edward Judge*	14
Grundy's Knowe *Clive Goodwin*	16
The Bowderstone Hut *Doug Blackett and Jeff Breen*	17
Walks from the Bowderstone *Hedley Smith*	24
Some Northumbrian Climbing Guides *Norman Haighton*	26
Six Decades of the Club *Stephen Porteus*	29
On the Snow Peak *Bob Hutchinson*	36
The Wind, Hedgehope Hill, January 1993 *Martin Cooper*	37
Saturday's Widow *Joan Murley*	38
Working Class *Pete Kirton*	40
Northumberland Rock	57
Northumbrian Exertions *Keith Gregory*	59
Reflections *John Earl*	62
Northumberland's Lost Crag *Andy Birtwistle*	67
Stones on Simonside *Martin Cooper*	69
County Ethics *Dave Cuthbertson*	70
Geordies – Keepers of the County *Bob Smith*	73
First Among Equals, An Obsession *Hugh Harris*	77
Crag Lough *Hilary Porteus*	80
From Northumberland to K2 … and Back *Alan Hinkes*	82
Recent Developments, 1989 – 1994 *John Earl*	84
Access to the Secluded County *Heather and Nigel Jamieson*	86
Selected First Ascents List *Compiled by Steve Crowe*	88

INTRODUCTION

"There is no nobler country than that of Northumberland, as it rolls processionally northward to the Border in great waves of coloured and historic moorland, cresting upon the skyline into sudden and surprising crags, which crown for us the magnificent walking with admirable rock climbs."

So wrote the climber, writer and poet, Geoffrey Winthrop Young in his foreword to the first Northumberland Rock Climbing Guidebook in 1950. The title of this book is a deliberate misquotation of Winthrop Young's description of Northumberland, for so close are his words to the hearts of Northumbrian climbers that his foreword to the first guidebook has been re-printed in each of the guidebooks published since. The statement, "No Nobler County" encapsulates the feelings of many of us about the experience of climbing and mountaineering in England's most northerly county.

This book is a celebration of climbing in Northumberland and is published in the 50th year of the Northumbrian Mountaineering Club. The NMC wishes to celebrate its 50th anniversary with a book about the club's raison d'etre – rock climbing in Northumberland. From gymnastic boulder problems on delightful, roadside sandstone crags, to truly testing routes in wild moorland settings, to longer more traditional climbing in the Cheviots and on the Roman Wall, Northumberland offers the rock climber a paradise in miniature, a county studded with gems. What Northumberland may lack in scale, compared to other climbing areas, it makes up for in stature; the County is renowned for being home to some of the most demanding technical routes in the country.

But "No Nobler County" is not just a celebration of climbing in wild places. It is a tribute to many of the people who made the climbs possible, to those who have developed the crags over the years, putting up the routes which we enjoy today and documenting them in the guidebooks. It is also a celebration of the people who have been members of the Northumbrian Mountaineering Club over the past 50 years, people who have worked on club huts, produced newsletters, sat on committees and kept the club alive. A small number of the club's founder members are still active on the hills and in club affairs. It is to these people in particular that this book is dedicated.

The book is divided into two sections: a history of the NMC and, secondly, a collection of articles on Northumberland climbing. The first section documents the activities of the NMC from its formation in May 1945 to the present day. As a club, the NMC has never been as large or as prestigious a club as the Climber's Club or the Fell and Rock. It should, however, be proud of its achievements. Five major guidebooks to Northumberland and a number of supplements have been produced. The club has maintained a membership of a hundred or more for most of the years of its existence. It has maintained three separate huts during the course of its history, Antic Hay, The Knowe and The Bowderstone huts. As well as the first ascents of hundreds of routes in Northumberland, NMC members have made the first ascents of some very notable climbs elsewhere in the country, particularly in the Lake District. The publication of this book sees the club going through a particularly successful period in its history: the Bowderstone huts have recently had major renovations completed and are virtually fully booked throughout the year; meets are well attended; membership stands at close to 200 and during the winter of 1994–95 the club has, for the first time, organised a series of indoor climbing competitions at the Concordia Climbing Wall, Cramlington. Roll on the next 50 years!

The second section of the book has a broader focus, covering climbing in Northumberland over the past 50 years, with contributions from outside as well as inside the NMC. While there has been a marked change in emphasis in certain aspects of climbing over this period – Keith Gregory's assertion that it didn't matter (in the 1940s) WHO did the first ascent of a route would be shared by few today – some clear themes run through many of the articles. First, historically, Northumberland has been an area where first ascents were done in a traditional style and where ethics have still been considered important. Secondly, a fierce rivalry has existed between groups, especially when rivals come from across the 'borders', Scotland, Yorkshire and the Lake District. Thirdly, Northumberland has boasted a tradition of pushing the grades of new routes as hard as is possible, matching the hardest routes to be found elsewhere in the country (the consensus view is that Northumberland routes are seriously undergraded in any case!). This latter trend has been strongly reinforced by Malcolm Smith's achievements in 1994. It must be pointed out that this section of the book is not intended to be a comprehensive or definitive history of climbing in the county. Rather, this part of the book attempts to give some colour to the characters of names that will already be familiar as well as telling one or two stories which previously have travelled no further than the bar of The Millstone, South Gosforth.

You will find, in the pages of this book, Northumberland described in many different ways: the quiet county; the secluded county; the atmospheric county. To many of the contributors to this book Northumberland is also 'the secret county' – a place where we wish to keep at bay the outsiders, the raiders, the tourists, the people who will spoil the isolation and turn Northumberland into Stanage on a Sunday afternoon. Why, then, have we written this book ? In the end, I suppose, the answer to that question is that Northumberland is also a love affair. We love the places that are described and pictured here with an affection that will last much longer than 50 years. We hope you will too.

The conception of this book took place on a February day in 1990 on a walking trip in the Cheviot Hills. Tony Griffiths and I walked over Preston and Broadhope Hills from Dunsdale and later in the afternoon climbed up to the Bizzle in search of ice. There was none. It was one of those typical winter's days in the Cheviots; rounded hills brightly lit by the low rays of sun, a cold wind to remind us of the latitude and a dramatic landscape with not a soul in sight. We discussed the idea of whether a history of climbing in Northumberland could be written in time for the 50th anniversary of the NMC in 1995. Tony had his doubts, since what was known of the subject had already been recorded in the guidebooks and the earlier history of the Northumberland crags, unlike that of, say, Lakeland or North Wales, had never been written down.

No more happened until early 1993 when preparations were begun to celebrate the NMC's 50th anniversary. This time I suggested the idea of a book to the Club's committee. The idea met with approval, although with a slightly different format, and so began a period of phone calls, conversations, cajoling, persuading and bullying in order to unearth contributors. It must be some mark of the project's success that, by the autumn of 1994, people were ringing me to ask if they could contribute, others to enquire if they were too late! The end result is to be found in the pages in front of you. Happy reading.

Martin Cooper, April 1995

Acknowledgements

The compilation of this book has been a team effort and so thanks are due, first of all, to the contributors, whose efforts made the book possible and to those whose contributions we unfortunately could not find room for. Secondly, I would like to thank the NMC's 50th anniversary sub-committee who have been generous with their advice, constructive criticism and support over the past year: Rick Barnes, Andy Birtwistle, Steve Crowe, John Earl and Stephen Porteus.

For their help with illustrations and photographs we would like to thank Nigel Jamieson, Rennie Barnes and Stuart Prince. We are indebted to John Traynor for his advice on the production side.

We are grateful to the Trustees of the Tate Gallery for granting permission to reproduce Grimshaw's painting of The Bowderstone. Thanks must also go to my family: to Mary for her patience and to Ben, Hannah and Joseph, Northumberland climbers of the future.

Finally, we would like to thank the following companies for their generous sponsorship of this book: Phoenix; Berghaus; Sprayway; Mountain Ear, Reebok; Vaudee; and for their advance support of the book: L D Mountain Centre; Wild Trak; Wilderness Ways; Outdoor World; Four Seasons; Wild Spirit; Northumbria Mountain Sports; Rock and Run; and Waterstones.

Thanks, It's a Privilege
Bob Bell

Having the County as your playground is a great privilege – the case is easily made. Take a typical Wednesday night. You have spent an evening at Ravensheugh. Perhaps you have triumphed, perhaps you have been pushed aside. After all there are no soft touches here to cruise. No nice fingery flakes like Bowden. Just steep cracks, high-angled 'slabs' and rounded ledges which have you trying to remember something about coefficients of friction. As the night shades in, a line of mist drifts around the crag and the atmosphere builds. The huge amphitheatre below begins to grow in your consciousness. A grouse coughs and your attention is drawn to the skyline. To the left are the Clennell Hills with Scotland behind and the Coquet flowing out across your line of sight. Straight ahead is the dominant line of the Cheviot partnered by the hump of Hedgehope. Further right the land slides away to a plain and on to a suspicion of sea. Your trek off the crag is into a gloom thickened by woodland. The crunch of the track as you descend seems likely to disturb the high edge of Simonside buttresses arranged above you like Easter Island watchers. A deer springs a mutual surprise as your paths cross. Soon there will be the 'night-life' of Rothbury to cope with. Nothing too arduous, a pint at the Turk's Head will qualify, but you may have to cope with the local pipers next door practising like some metronomic swarm of bees.

But that's only a snapshot, a single example of what is on offer. So many other cards make up the pack of Northumberland experiences. The variety is truly astonishing and it is your great fortune to be able to shuffle the pack and deal to your heart's content. Roadside cragging at Bowden or Corby's can be balanced by visits to remoter eyries like Ravensheugh or Coe. Surprising gems like Berryhill and Selby's Cove complement the great popular edges at Simonside and the Wanney. Huge walking expeditions can be strung together around Windy Gyle, Bloodybush Edge, Cushat Law and all the skyline of Alwinton. Great winter horseshoes can be formed around the College and Langlee valleys. The Tors behind Cheviot can be linked to form a rim around Commonburn House with views into every corner of the northern Cheviots and across the Till plain to the sea. From all of this you will get great variety of scenery, but always there will be linking themes of huge skies and limited human traffic generating a heady mix of isolation and euphoria.

Yet your self-induced solitude is constantly tripped by lumps of history which can't be avoided. Castles and keeps are only the obvious evidence of politics and high intrigue. Set at less portentous levels are the poignant stoney heaps of deserted villages, the unsuspected cleughs and coves of the reivers and those stunning examples of faith carved in spirals on the rocks by who knows who. Even as you walk across a bare hillside your path lies on a product managed by and for the waves of sheep who have washed away the scrub and straggle of the original upland. Every top has its bronze age circle and the levels often yield burial cists, old furnaces and sites of hearths. A great network of trails for drovers, salters and thieves lies across and links all the favourite remote corners of this 'quiet' county. Perhaps our present gift of space is a modern phenomenon and the reality of Bronze Age and Mediaeval Northumberland was that you were never out of sight of your neighbour.

On a short day a modest outing can be traced out along the coast, or the Wall, or on the moor above Old Bewick which stretches up past Kyloe and holds the waters around Wooler from reaching the sea, sending them North to the Tweed. Tackle the County's moorland from any direction you like except where grouse are pampered or where there is uncomfortable accommodation with the MOD between Otterburn and Alwinton. Sandstone tors pop out everywhere carrying traces of peregrine and jackdaw. Somehow each outing seems to yield a gem. It may be spotting a file of goats threading their way around the western flank of Yeavering Bell, or pausing above Crag Lough while snipe thrum the air and swans court on the fringe of the lake.

A diet solely made up of atmosphere would deaden most palates and so in the interest of fairness, the existence must be confirmed of widespread indulgence in great communal climb and banter sessions. Sunny dusty days at Bowden either bouldering or fiddling with some route that's too hard are a great delight.

They can be matched by similar time wasting events in the woods at Kyloe doing starts and bits of traverses laced with plenty of nips from the flask and the exchange of detailed, highly personal character assassinations.

But what keeps pulling you back from lay-offs and rushes at work and dicky elbows and marital arm-locks isn't just fun or athletics. It's a bit more to do with space and the presence you feel on the best of days. As all the commentators say, it is the quiet county. But it is also the big county and the atmospheric county. Try walking off Coe Crag at dusk. A curlew whistles you out and your last look at the north west captures the Cheviot backlit with a sun that's well down but not dead. Try not to be impressed – it won't work.

The Northumbrian Mountaineering Club
1945 – 1995

Early NMC climbers on Hadrian's Buttress, Crag Lough. Photograph: Angus McDonald.

NMC Presidents
1945 – 1995

1945 – 1947	Dr Emrys Williams	1969 – 1970	Stuart Miller
1947 – 1949	Frank Oakes-Smith	1970 – 1971	Clive Goodwin
1949 – 1952	Dr A B L Levy	1972 – 1975	Geoff Jackson
1952 – 1955	Claud Bicknell	1975 – 1977	John Earl
1955 – 1956	Basil Butcher	1977 – 1979	Stephen Porteus
1956 – 1957	Bill Robson	1979 – 1982	Tony Griffiths
1957 – 1958	Dennis Hall	1982	Jeff Breen
1958 – 1959	Robert Conn	1982	Norman Haighton
1959 – 1960	M G D Johnson	1983 – 1984	Hilary Porteus
1960 – 1961	J Wolfe	1984 – 1985	Tony Griffiths
1961 – 1963	Don Barr-Wells	1985 – 1987	Robin Sillem
1963 – 1964	John Porter	1987 – 1989	Andy Birtwistle
1964 – 1965	Jim Robinson	1989 – 1991	Bob Bell
1965 – 1966	Gordon Mitchell	1991 – 1993	Nigel Jamieson
1966 – 1967	Doreen Walden	1993 – 1995	Rick Barnes
1967 – 1968	J Donaldson	1995 –	Steve Crowe
1968 – 1969	Norman Haighton		

Club meet, Crag Lough, 1940s.

The Formation of the NMC and Its Early Years
Martin Cooper and Angus McDonald

At an informal meeting at King's College, Newcastle upon Tyne, on 31st May 1945, 46 years after the first recorded rock climb in Northumberland, the Northumbrian Mountaineering Club was founded. The activities of the club in its early days were well documented. A reading of the minutes of committee meetings and of Annual General Meetings and of the early club bulletins show a keen, energetic and dedicated group of people who were active on the crags, hills and mountains of this country as well as abroad. This introductory article paints a picture of the activities of the early NMC members and details the early evolution of the club.

The Northumbrian Mountaineering Club had in fact first been formed in 1942 following two accidents on Crag Lough. It was almost immediately disbanded as many of its members left to join the forces. Although some climbing in Northumberland did continue during the war years, it was the end of the war in 1945 which saw the beginning of the present club. A number of the founder members had been members of the King's College Climbing Club; the climbing activities of the founder members were centred on Crag Lough, where routes such as Pinnacle Face, Main Wall, Hadrian's Wall and Grad's Groove had already been established by the 1940's. It was not surprising, therefore, that Crag Lough was chosen as the venue for the first NMC meet on 23rd June 1945. A second meet was scheduled for August Bank Holiday 1945 in Langdale.

Minutes from the first meeting show that of the original 29 members of the club eight were engineers, six were students, three university lecturers, three draughtsmen, three civil servants and amongst the others, a journalist, a builder, and a chemist. The club's initial appeal was wide. By August of 1945 a further 14 local climbers had applied to join. By 1949 the club had nearly 100 members. Rules drafted for the club at its initial meetings were very straightforward, covering constitution, subscriptions, objectives of the club and meetings. The original subscription was 10s-6d a year. The objective of the club was "to promote mountaineering in Northumberland".

Crag Lough continued to be the favourite crag of the club in its early years. Steps were taken almost immediately to secure accommodation for club members nearby when Basil Butcher offered to change the tenancy of his cottage, later known as "Antic Hay", so that it could be used by the club. Founder member Angus McDonald recalls that a local farmer declared war on wood pigeons one summer, erecting long wooden troughs filled with poisoned corn above the scree slopes at the bottom of Crag Lough. "Often when climbing, when one reached for an obscured hold on a hidden ledge or in a hidden crack we would put our hands into a mass of decaying bird. Our clothes and ropes developed a distinctive odour, "Crag Lough smell". Tony Hopkins' National Trail Guide to the Northern section of the Pennine Way describes Crag Lough as a rock face of Whin Sill where "vertical chasms in the rock face add a hint of danger which should be negotiated with care". Nothing deterred the early NMC climbers at Crag Lough. By the end of the 1940's 46 routes had been pioneered on the crag.

Only three other Northumbrian crags were visited regularly by club members in the period up to 1950: The Wanneys, Simonside and the Henhole. The first guidebook, which appeared in 1950, covered Crag Lough, The Wanneys and Simonside only. An inspection of the railway map of Northumberland from this time explains why. With petrol rationing continuing after the war – in any case only one of the founder members had a car – the only way to get to the crags was by public transport – train to Rothbury for Simonside, to Bellingham for the Wanneys and Bardon Mill for Crag Lough. The crags of the Cheviot area, Henhole, The Bizzle and Dunsdale were occasionally visited, transport being by bus and by foot.

Because of the distance to be covered from railway stations to the crags, not to mention the infrequency of trains, climbing trips necessitated an overnight stay. For the Wanneys this would be at the Youth Hostel at Bellingham (a fair walk away) or bivouacking amongst the boulders or, if it was wet, under the railway arch on the line between Woodburn and Knowesgate. At Simonside members usually camped. At Crag Lough, of course, club members had their own hut, "Antic Hay" and later "Grundy's Knowe". For the Cheviot, the club had a permanently erected tent.

When NMC members decided to climb further afield the effort required would have daunted the spirits of all but the most enthusiastic modern climbers. For Angus to visit the Lakes for a climbing weekend he would have to take a day and a half off work (Friday afternoon and Saturday), travel by train from South Shields to Newcastle, from Newcastle to Carlisle, from Carlisle to Penrith, and change yet again, from Penrith to Keswick where he would hitch a lift along Borrowdale and walk up to Sty Head Tarn, to camp by ten o'clock on Friday night. This would give a whole day's climbing on the Saturday but it was necessary to be back at Keswick by four pm on Sunday to catch the last train home.

Tedious waits at railway stations usually resulted in high level traverses round the waiting room or impromptu Scottish dances on the station platform, much to the amusement of fellow passengers, accompanied by Edwin Scott-Elcoat on his pipes. Meals would be cooked in train compartments on primus stoves and the tradition was that the last meal of a meet would be a shared one, with members contributing whatever they had left to be cooked, in a large dixie.

Climbing equipment in the immediate post war era was rudimentary, to say the least. Ropes were of Italian Hemp, hawser laid and exceedingly stiff when wet. Angus's first rope cost £7-10s-0d. He remembers the climbing methods which early NMC members used – a long way from "Red Points" and "French Style". Belaying, as known today, didn't exist. The rope was tied directly round the waist. Careful climbers would carry one sling. Angus sometimes carried two. Protection was virtually non-existent. Occasionally a sling could be slipped behind a wedged chockstone but the only way to attach the rope was by untying, putting the rope through the sling and tying on again. Karabiners were very scarce, usually ex-army and not generally available.

Footwear was normally ex-army boots with either ring clinkers or tricouni nails. The wearing of "rubbers" was considered cheating. One member of the club made himself a special pair of boots for climbing in Skye with numerous small aluminium blocks secured onto the soles, excellent for friction on the Gabbro rock. The first NMC trip to Skye, in 1946, is remembered by Angus for teaching members a lesson in climbing technique. War time diet meant that climbers were lean and fit, with a good power to body weight ratio. At home in Northumberland they could happily pull up on a hold with one arm, and did so. The rough rock of the Cuillin soon shredded the North East climber's fingers and a lesson was learned in using the feet properly on holds. Clothing had been on ration in the war so, again, there were no specially designed clothes for the NMC pioneers. They wore army surplus clothing, anoraks and shortened trench coats.

In the 50 year period since the formation of the NMC certain things have not changed. The original club members soon sorted themselves out into committee types, enthusiasts and, as Angus remembers, "the elite climbers" – those who wore rubbers and could climb severes. There were also, of course, larger than life characters. Edwin Scott Elcoat had been a piper in the Black Watch. Early club photographs show that he wore his kilt to meets and he rarely went anywhere without his pipes. Teddy Hertrich was a pork butcher and, like Corporal Jones of "Dad's Army", could somehow get around the rationing rules. Angus remembers that he always brought two things to meets: his dry sense of humour and plenty of sausages – at club meets he would comment "We've had the Stone Age, the Bronze Age, the Iron Age and now we've got the Saus-age" pulling yards of sausage from his pack.

Jack Pickford was above all else, an enthusiast. He was club treasurer, led meets, illustrated the Simonside section for the first guide and, Angus recalls, would climb irrespective of the weather, having in particular, a penchant for wet gullies. In the winter of 1946–47, Jack Pickford and Angus played an unforgettable part in a ski-rescue at Allendale. 1946–47 was one of the hardest winters in living memory. The NMC were called upon to help rescue the outlying farms and the township of Allenheads, which had been cut off by snow for six weeks. Of the 18 NMC members who took part Jack Pickford and Angus McDonald were the most competent skiers, having just returned from two weeks in Norway. They were given the task of delivering food parcels to the most distant farms. However, the depth of the snow and the distance to be covered meant that Pickford and McDonald did not arrive back at Allendale until late at night, by which time their own food and sleeping bags were locked away in the General Store. The store keeper could not be contacted; the rest of the NMC party had long since departed for the hut at Crag Lough. The two intrepid rescuers had to break into a barn where they shivered the night away in sub-zero temperatures.

The club's first committee were clearly a diligent group of individuals. Dr Emrys Williams was president, Frank Oakes-Smith vice president. Basil Butcher and Peggie Robinson joint secretaries, Pickford treasurer and the original committee members were Edwin Elcoat, Arthur Edmonson, Chris Waters (the Chris Waters of Kinlochleven Fell and Rock hut), A R Hutchinson, Dennis Hall, F G Morris and Dorothy Golding Smith. Reading through the minutes of meetings held between 1945 and 1950 one becomes aware that many of the present traditions of the club were established in those early years and that many of the concerns of club members are no different to those of members 50 years ago. The first AGM was held in October 1945 when the BMC was informed of the club's existence. The first Annual Dinner took place in February 1946 at the Fox and Hounds, Bardon Mill. At the committee meeting of 26th November 1945 the committee were asked to sanction the buying of a dozen mattresses for the hut at Crag Lough. The minutes state, "It was sanctioned, but against the wishes of Mr F Oakes-Smith who contended that they would be continuously damp and impair the health of the members who used them" (the mattresses at the Bowderstone have done much the same for the past 20 years!). The idea of a guide book was first raised in May 1946. At the same time a sub-committee was formed in order to decide upon the most suitable type of paper to use for club correspondence!

At a committee meeting in 1946 the winter lecturers were inaugurated. The relative formality of club proceedings at this time may be judged from the following extract from the minutes of a meeting on 9th January 1947 – "Annual Dinner to be held at the Fox and Hounds, Bardon Mill, on 18th January 1947. Mr F Oakes-Smith has kindly arranged to give a lantern lecture on the Outer Hebrides after the dinner, also to supply a few bottles of sherry which would be paid for by the members of the club".

The first club Bulletin – now known as the club newsletter – came out early in 1949. Already at this time the club were looking backwards as well as forwards. An article entitled, "Preliminary notes on the History of Northumberland Rock Climbing" appeared in the first Bulletin, as well as an account of the first girdle traverse of Crag Lough Central Buttress by B J Cooke, and an article about the legendary Borrowdale climbing character, Millican Dalton. Apparently Dalton had once climbed Napes Needle with a friend, hauled up a bundle of firewood, with which he lit a fire on top of the needle to boil his coffee.

There was some debate in early Bulletins about the clubs raison d'etre. More specifically, the question was raised: should the NMC provide training for new and prospective members? The word "evangelism" is even used. A few meets each year were designated Novices meets. For example at Simonside, May 1940 – "The meet was attended by 18 members, including seven novices. The weather was good and ten of us camped at the old site. Most of the climbing was done on the Sunday when the novices were put to the easy climbs on the Simonside Crags. Mr Levy took charge of the abseiling using the safety line for the new starters. "This meet report also recounts the author, RWR having trouble in climbing the "only unled climb in that district" – from the description, obviously Long Layback Crack.

The early Bulletins show club members as being active in a wide range of mountaineering pursuits, both in Britain and abroad. Bulletins from 1949 contain reports of the following exploits: climbs and scrambles around Zermatt; a report of a visit to Switzerland where attempts were made on the Mettlehorn, Alpine climbing in Austria and France; walking trips, including moonlit walks in the Pennines and Cheviots; rock climbing in Northumberland; camping and bivouacking in the Peak District and the Cairngorms and a delightful account of a climbing weekend at Borrowdale at Easter.

A few lines from the last mentioned report gives a flavour of what climbing was like for NMC members 50 years ago. The author was B J Cooke. "We will not forget Raven Crag Gully very easily. There was quite a lot of water and it could not very well be avoided. We all emerged from the top of the first pitch as though we had just been fished out of deep water in full climbing kit ... in contrast Black Crag Buttress (Troutdale Pinnacle) was climbed in rubbers in brilliant sunshine. We revelled in the fine exposure of the pinnacle, but the leader was grateful for a running belay in surmounting the main difficulty of the last pitch ... Gillercombe – Jack Pickford did not fancy the buttress so he spent the morning moving on and off the cliff at different levels. I must say it was encouraging, after a hard pitch, suddenly to see his head and shoulders 50 feet higher on the skyline. We were mistaken in doing the climb in boots; rubbers would have been more enjoyable. However, we shared the leads and running belays made my share seem safer. We reached the top, shouting for Jack, when we suddenly saw him just at our feet waking from a deep sleep."

So, The Northumbrian Mountaineering Club was born, not as a club with burning ambition, nor as a club which would make great headlines in the climbing world, but as an amalgamation of like minded people in Northumberland, dedicated to climbing and mountaineering.

NMC Alpine Meet, Zermatt, 1947.
Photograph: Muriel Sauer.

Great Gable, Christmas 1944
Edward Judge

Rarely can some important event be attributed to one cause; usually it is a concatenation of minor circumstances which leads to the fulfilment of an ideal, or of a disaster. Sometimes the circumstances themselves are collectively insufficient and another factor, often unexpected, brings about a change of great import. Such, I believe, was the case in the formation of the Northumbrian Mountaineering Club in 1945.

From time to time during the previous year, usually around the fire in the youth hostel after a day on the hill, there was talk of a climbing club, but it never amounted to much and the idea found little support. There were only a few of us, we tended to climb with the same partners, enjoyed the solitude and the peace of our surroundings and were wary, even fearful, of anything which might disturb the delightful environment which was so dear to us. And so we continued happily until the end of the year when a tragedy rocked our little world.

On Christmas Eve 1944 Sid Walker and I came up out of Borrowdale onto Sty Head, traversed across the south face of Great Gable to the Napes, and climbed the Needle Ridge. We were followed closely by Raymond Coulthard and Myra (Bunty) Williams on a separate rope. It was a bad day, the rocks were cold to the touch, and we were enveloped in cloud. At the top of the climb we huddled together for a few minutes against the cold wind and then prepared to descent, Raymond and Myra by the Eagle's

Northumberland climbing group, The Wanneys, September 1944. Myra Williams is on the right of the second row from the back. Edward Judge is on the extreme left of the front row. Photograph: Muriel Sauer.

Nest ridge, Sid and myself by the Arrowhead. We moved off and immediately lost sight of one another until, about the level of the strid, a window opened in the cloud enabling Myra and myself to see each other, but neither could see anyone else. She stood just above where the ridge falls steeply, with rope running up into the cloud to Raymond above. We exchanged a few words, then the window closed up as she gave a rather forlorn wave. A few seconds later they fell. The noise was terrible, our climb down to them nerve-racking, the scene in the Needle Gully where they lay dead was ghastly. Carrying them across the steep face was far from easy, especially as it was dark before we reached Sty Head, and the wartime blackout restrictions forbad out using torches. In the following days we had the distressing tasks of trying to console the heart-broken parents, giving evidence at the inquest, and carrying our friends to their grave at Stonethwaite Churchyard. When I returned home at New Year my parents were surprised to see that my hair had turned grey.

Our small group of climbers was stunned by the catastrophe. It was very hard to realise that our friends were gone. Some, like Myra's brother, Harry, never climbed again, and others distanced themselves from a pastime in which the consequences could be so devastating. A psychological gloom seemed to descend on the crags, gone was the delightful, happy chatter, replaced by a seemingly inexplicable tension. I found it hard to regain form, and I remember clearly having to retreat from a route at Crag Lough I'd climbed many times, while a young Angus MacDonald, watched from below, hung his head at my distress, and muttered, "Sad, sad".

We recovered, perhaps not completely, and emerged with a heightened awareness of each other, and with a need for a focal point on which to concentrate our thoughts and so give us unity. It may have been no more than a wish to fortify ourselves. Within a few weeks the NMC was founded.

"It is an ill wind turns none to good."

*Picnic at Crag Lough,
Raymond Coulthard on the right.*

Grundy's Knowe
Clive Goodwin

I remember turning up at my first Knowe working meet where my skills as a mixer of cement and plaster were carefully noted by committee members. Graham Townsend was warden and the two separate rooms were suddenly launched into one with huge open fires at each end. We were able to burn not just logs but whole trees! The Knowe faced south but can be seen on a hill just south of the Housesteads car park on the Bardon Mill road. Climbing was done on Crag Lough and later Peel Crag. Drinking was nearly always included in at the Bowes in Bardon Mill and how we ever drove home to the hut in the pre-breathaliser days without mishaps I do not know. High jinks followed as they still do but a visit to the Elsan toilet a hundred yards away subdued even the highest of spirits. One famous party night was so packed out that the last one into the upstairs communal dormitory had to sleep on the trap door, only to endure a sleepless night as weak bladders took their toll.

Graham moved to Hull after fitting calor gas cooking and I was made hut warden at an emergency committee meeting held at the fell and rock hut, Bracken Close, in Wasdale in 1963. I, with friends, installed the calor gas lighting and a huge wine barrel for rain water. Later I managed to persuade the committee to install a self flushing chemical loo but unfortunately it never worked due to people forever adding "foreign bodies" to it. Our well was there but it had been used for dumping paint tins and refuse for years. We used the cable trough sometimes and distant springs but the lack of a water supply always led to cleaning problems when the warden wasn't there. The original hut had a grass sod roof, I am told, and was given to the club in its early days by a Haltwistle landowner on a peppercorn rent. Local people told us how "Ard Grundy" had hanged himself there and a builder confirmed this and even showed me the roof beam used!

Sadly as cars made Crag Lough a day meet crag clubs use grew less, yet when the roof blew off in the mid 60's following a storm we decided to renew this. All the old asbestos sheets were buried outside and a new roof, new floor and new bunks were made whist Jim Robinson was president. The workmanship was superb and Jack Donaldson and Vic Johnson who did most of the internal joinery transferred their skills both to the Bowderstone.

The Knowe was kept on after we moved to the lakes but eventually another storm blew in the gable end and we then gave it back to the landowner. The hut fund was financed by jumble sales held at Snow Street School off Westgate Road!

In the quest for a Lakeland hut we looked at a mine building near the Youth Hostel in Glenridding. Then we put in plans to convert a pig sty in Rosthwaite opposite the Village Hall or Institute. Finally we discovered the Bowderstone and asked the National Trust if we could rent this. At first they seemed to agree but suddenly it was placed on the market for other clubs to put in a bid. We deliberately sent Don Barr-Wells and Gordon Mitchell to charm Mr Aclands, the administrator, at a site meeting and these gentlemen succeeded in clinching the cottage which we still have. Our first New Year party there was marvellous with candles in the nearly empty cottage. One sad reflection on club huts is that those who built the interiors and looked after them definitely gave up many weekends month after month when they should have been out on the crags.

The Bowderstone Hut

For nearly 30 years the NMC has been fortunate enough to have its own hut in the Lake District, Bowderstone Cottage in Borrowdale, leased since 1966 from the National Trust. The cottage was built at the end of the 18th century by local landowner Joseph Pocklington, within a stone's throw of the Bowderstone rock, "for an old woman to live in who is to show the rock, for fear travellers should pass under it without seeing it". The Bowderstone itself was already a tourist attraction in the 18th century; Pocklington was the first to erect a ladder against it. The poet, Robert Southey, friend of Wordsworth and Coleridge, wrote in 1807.

"Another mile of broken ground, the most interesting which I ever traversed, brought us to a single rock called the Bowder Stone, a fragment of great size which has fallen from the heights. The same person (ie: Mr Pocklington) who formerly disfigured the island in Keswick Lake with so many abominations, has been at work here also; has built a little mock hermitage, set up a new druidical stone, erected an ugly house for an old woman to live in who is to show the rock, for fear travellers should pass under it without seeing it, cleared away all the fragments round it, and as it rests upon a narrow base, like a ship upon its keel, dug a hole underneath through which the curious may gratify themselves by shaking hands with the old woman. The oddity of this amused us greatly, provoking as it was to meet with such hideous buildings in such a place – for the place is as beautiful as eyes can behold or imagination conceive."

Southey was wrong with his geology; the Bowderstone is in fact an erractic glacial boulder. Most modern Lakeland tourists would agree, however, with his description of the beauty spot. NMC members would disagree wholeheartedly with Southey's description of the cottage and hermitage as hideous. For these two huts, for many years, have meant more to NMC members than just the happy hours spent there. Doug Blackett tells the story of the NMC's association with the Bowderstone from initial negotiations with the National Trust through to the mid 1970's. Jeff Breen brings the story forward to the present day.

Bowderstone History
Doug Blackett

It was in the Summer of 1964 when four members of the Knowe work party, who were busy refurbishing the cottage after a series of harsh gales, stumbled upon their future. Behind the trees lay Bowderstone Cottage, and the possibility that the 90 members of the Northumbrian Mountaineering Club would be able to house their own meets. Beautifully situated in the heart of Borrowdale, Bowerstone Cottage became the new focus for the NMC. The bare shell of the cottage would need extensive work on it, if it was to reach a habitable level, without electricity, water, a septic tank and easy access by car, the cottage was not going to be refurbished overnight. Although the work was going to be a lengthy process the good foundations, and beautiful position of the cottage, laid the base for the NMC's new home in Borrowdale.

Correspondence between the NMC and the National Trust was opened up, and from August 1965 Hilda Bath was in contact with Mr Aclands. Hilda Bath and Vic Jonson negotiated the National Trust and Lake District Planning board into an eventual agreement with help coming from unusual quarters.

Captain S H Bradrock of The Scafell Hotel in Rosthwaite who was on the committee for the National Trust, lent his support for the NMC's cause. Such well placed support was certainly needed, with there being some 40 other applicants for the cottage. The conclusion of the year long correspondence with the National Trust and Lake District Planning Board, was eventual acquisition of a seven year lease. On the 24th of June 1966 the cottage became part of the NMC's future and history was being made.

Expectations rose, and with the chance to own their own hut in the Lake District, which may never have occurred again, people were stimulated into action. Doreen Walden, and Gordon Mitchell began the work by establishing a hut appeal. Costs were high, and with funds already committed to the equipping of the Knowe a new source of money was needed. Basic improvements on Bowderstone Cottage were to cost around £200, which unfortunately coincided with the restoration of the Knowe after the harsh gales of 1964. The formation of the hut appeal in November of 1965 was, therefore, only a beginning, as even today the need for money to maintain Bowderstone Cottage continues.

The Club's resident architect, Vic Jonson, began the mammoth task of organising the renovations as soon as the lease was obtained. Contact was set up between the NMC and local Keswick builders to obtain tenders for the proposed work, while Vic Jonson negotiated the National Trust, and Lake District Planning Board into an agreement. On the 4th of September 1966 a quote arrived which satisfied the NMC and it was this quote from Mr Bainbridge which was finally accepted. The estimated cost was around £340 and Mr Bainbridge was given the all clear to start on the renovations. Unfortunately, work was held up by the Borrowdale floods of September 1966, and it was a while before work could begin. Eventually Mr Bainbridge supplied the cottage with new plumbing, sanitary fittings, doors, partitions, and drainage to the septic tank.

The NMC finally had a base to house their meets and moved into Bowderstone Cottage. Although the fundamental improvements at the Bowderstone had been completed, the cottage was not fully functional, and it was not until the 26th of September 1966 when the major restoration began. The primary task was to fit the cottage with a new kitchen and bunks, and it was the sleeping arrangements where the first stumbling block arose. The National Trust forbade the mixed sleeping set-up, and conventions of the time required that a chastity curtain was needed to divide the sexes. Hilda Bath immediately solved the problem by purchasing an immense quantity of curtain material and joining it together. The solution was found; a curtain pinned up to divide the room, and, therefore, the sexes. The delivery of timber to fit out the cottage was also far from plain sailing. Edmund Robson was organised to deliver the timber, but an unfortunate series of punctures resulted in an impromptu overnight camp out. While the truck carrying the timber was repaired, the driver slept in the cab, and Douglas Blackett spent a wet night under the truck.

The building of the Green Westmorland slate fireplace resulted from a clandestine visit to Honister quarry. Good quality Lakeland slate was gathered from all available sources, the most prominent of which was Honister quarry. Jack Donaldson, Vic Jonson, and Clive Goodwin extracted the slate, but they did so with the help of an insider. John the quarryman aided and abetted these illicit slate gathering trips.

The main problem for the Bowderstone refurbishers was supplying the cottage with a fundamental necessity – water. Initially, water was obtained from a small spring in the back garden, which fed the storage tank. By the second day of a meet, however, the water supply would run out and club members could be seen scurrying down the hillside in search of water. One day in the Scafell Hotel it was heard that there was a water source about 300 yards up the hillside from the hut. The work party set forth to investigate the rumour and discovered that a mineshaft did hold clean water. Success! Steps were then taken to pipe the water down to the cottage and although it was a lengthy process the end result was clean and quenched club members.

While work was well on course on the Bowderstone Cottage attention was turned to the Hermitage. The empty shell of the Hermitage was stripped out, and the set pot boiler was removed by Derek Craggs and Ian Turnbull. The roof and walls required attention before the Hermitage was even fitted out, and the work party spent an uncomfortable night on the old wooden baton doors after concreting the floor. Les Rimmer supervised the making of the window frames and the building of the first floor. Again the club found assistance from outsiders, with Formica kindly donating the chipboard for the new first floor of the Hermitage. The work on the cottage and the Hermitage laid the foundations for future refurbishment, but it was only the beginning. A programme of continuous improvements had begun with a culmination in a series of major works in the 1970's. By the 1970's the cottage was being extensively used by visiting clubs, which exacerbated the need to upgrade the fittings. The old canvas bunks were replaced with a new three tier system, the kitchen fittings, cooker and work tops were all replaced, and the gas lighting was overhauled and modernised. Even the ceiling in the main room was lowered to maximise the heating of the cottage. The Hermitage too benefited from a refit between 1972–74 and acquired new bunks. The transportation of the foam rubber for the new bunks holds a story on its own. Dr John Elliot's minibus was used to transport the foam rubber and it was so full that Tom Hammill had hardly room to move while driving.

The comradeship felt between club members encouraged a feeling of kind spirited and good hearted fun. Early working meets, therefore, enjoyed a very good attendance from club members and their friends. The extensive work done on the refurbishment of Bowderstone Cottage, and the Hermitage, strangely enough coincided with the consumption of much ale. The frequent visits to the Scafell bred a close relationship with Bill the publican, and resulted in his donation of a kitchen table, which is still used after 20 years. As long as the Northumbrian Mountaineering Club has the use of Bowderstone Cottage so the frequent trips to The Scafell will continue and, hopefully, the natural enjoyment of the meets will always exist.

The Bowderstone Hut. Photograph: Stuart Prince.

Bringing the Bowderstone Hut into the Twentieth Century
Jeff Breen

In 1976 Tom Hammill became hut warden. Tom brought a new urgency to the job and was responsible for the start of the modern revival of Bowderstone Cottage. Tom, a one time shipyard worker turned Maths teacher, gave a new-found humour and practicality to cottage maintenance meets. His humour and friendliness resulted in working meets actually becoming a popular event in the club calendar.

Tom, with his practical eye, saw that the Bowderstone Hut needed essential building from the bottom up. Most club members will not appreciate the amount of work that Tom did, often alone or with a small group of friends. His first job was restoring the water supply from the mine and building a header tank in the garden. His next and most important project was the sewerage system. The cesspit was very old and in a state of collapse, and as a result, was polluting the river. Tom rebuilt this virtually from scratch. The gas system was then extensively renovated and we switched from butane to propane in 1978. This allowed the installation of hot water heaters in both huts.

Halfway through Tom's wardenship a major problem arose – dry rot was discovered beneath the floor of the cottage. Lesser men might have given up but Tom systematically lifted all the flooring and removed affected plasters from the walls. He then filled in the large void below the floors with rubble and finally concreted over the top, and replastered the walls. This was a project comparable with the building of the pyramids at Giza, and the Great Wall of China, all in the same weekend. Tom continued as hut warden till 1983 when he retired, leaving the legacy of a dramatically improved hut.

Before Tom rebuilt the water system, it had regularly failed, usually in drought conditions, which meant one had to walk up to the source of supply. This was a horizontal mine shaft, or level, running deep into the hillside high above the hut. The level is usually about one foot deep in water, which is drawn from the mine using a syphon. When the syphon failed, one person had to go into the mine to retrieve the pipe. This was then filled with water outside the mine, and one luckless volunteer had to climb back down the level with his thumb over the pipe and thrust it in the water at the same time as yelling to his mate outside to open the valve. This created a 500 foot head of suction and you had to be quick to remove your thumb, or else lose it. One day this fairly routine procedure was being enacted. Tom was outside and his sidekick, Paul Selley, was inside the mine with the pipe. Tom then heard a loud rumble and turned to see a telephone box sized block of rock and assorted debris collapse across the mine entrance. Panic ensued, but after frantic digging a rather shaken Paul Selley was extricated from his predicament.

It was not long after this that Tom had cause to be grateful for rescuing his friend alive. Our two heroes were climbing Moss Ghyll Grooves on Scafell Crag. Tom took a long leader fall and finally ended up back on the belay ledge with a dislocated elbow. A FRCC team climbing nearby alerted the rescue services. Meanwhile Tom was suffering from shock. Paul, naturally concerned, put his anorak around Tom and tried to zip it up. Unfortunately the zip jammed. Forcing the zip his hand slipped off and he smacked Tom full in the face and gave him a bloody nose. The rescue team, on arrival, assessed Tom's condition, strapped his arm and asked "What about your nose?". Tom replied, "Oh my friend did that".

In 1983 Jeff Breen took over the wardenship of the cottage. Tom's was a hard act to follow. Jeff, aided and abetted by his wife Lynne, decided to attract more members to working meets. Bribes were laid on, such as free beer in the hut on the Saturday night and free lunch during the day. It worked. Punters came from far and wide and meets reached the heady heights of 30 plus members on occasion. Many a drunken climber sustained injury on the Bowderstone in the wee small hours.

Ten days before the November 1988 working meet it became apparent that a new roof was needed for the cottage kitchen. A new roof was costed out on the coffee table, a quick ring around for money from the treasurer and for volunteers and the next day materials were ordered for the working meet.

By Friday night Tom McGuinness had removed all the old slates and had taken delivery of all the materials. Saturday had the job well under way, with the new roof timbers being fitted. Then we had a problem. The walls soaked with damp caused by the leaking roof were crumbling. Soon we had lost about two feet off the top. An urgent convoy of cars was organised and sent to Cockermouth for sand and cement. This was followed by some strenuous aerobic exercise carrying it all up the track. Eventually the walls were stabilised and the work could continue. Sunday saw the roof timbers in place and the felting added, just as it started to snow. The inside of the cottage was like a disaster area and it took a full week to get it back into usable order. Ventilators were installed and the roof retiled by Johnny Douglas on his week's holiday.

Things quietened down after this and working meets became more routine. It was on one of these meets that the hut warden, after spending too long in the Scafell bar, suggested a moonlit ascent of Central Gully. "Been reading too much W H Murray", someone was heard to say. Anyway the bluff was called and midnight saw a merry party of four well on their way to the crag. It was cold and there was a full moon. Halfway up Tom's crampon fell apart and we spent about an hour fixing it. "Don't worry", someone said "the worst that can happen is that we will be bedayed". Eventually we topped out to an unforgettable view of the Scafells by moonlight.

Working on the hut it became increasingly apparent, that if we were to improve it any further then we needed electricity. This had been suggested many years before but was regarded as too expensive.

The club committee agreed that if we could get a new 21 year lease from the National Trust for the cottage then it would be worthwhile to invest in the hut and install electricity. With approval from the National Trust a contract was drawn up with Norweb, with the club to do most of the preparatory work. The cost would be £12,500. Our first task was to dig two trenches from a point in the back garden of the cottage. One cable would go across the track to the smaller cottage and the other about 40 feet to the main cottage. It took a day to dig the trenches, lay the ducting and backfill the trenches. Easy, we thought. By Sunday morning at breakfast all we had to do was knock two holes for cables into the main cottage. Musing over his muesli, Nigel Jamieson said "Jeff, why do we need two holes into the cottage?" Jeff replied "One for each cable you dozey so and so." "Two cables" blustered Nigel, "But we've only laid one!". All eyes turned to Jeff: "Now lads, calm down". Murder was on the cards. The short 40 foot trench was redug that day and two ducts laid. Jeff narrowly avoided being buried with them.

Time passed as we waited for Norweb to get planning permission for their overhead cable and transformer. Shortly before the meeting of the Allerdale Council planning committee, we received a letter from the National Trust. They had misread Norweb's plans and had not realised that the installation involved an overhead cable and that it was their policy for all cables to go underground. So the very next day at the planning department's meeting the National Trust actually objected to their own planning application! As a result of this fiasco Norweb then had to resubmit new plans for the system to go completely underground, and these were passed.

Thankfully the National Trust agreed they were at fault and were responsible for the extra work. Then much to our delight an unexpected bonus came our way. As the run of cable was now much shorter than before, Norweb informed us that the cost would now come down to £7,500 This was nearly a third of the original quotation. Luck was on our side.

"What do you mean, there should have been two cables!" Jeff Breen's great cabling cock-up, Bowderstone Cottage electrification.

At last all the major problems were solved, or so we thought. The National Trust relayed the ducting and we asked Norweb to mark out the position of the transformer plinth, which they duly did, but in the wrong place!

Finally Norweb installed the system, tested our internal electrics, and by Christmas 1991 we were connected to the national grid. While Norweb and the National Trust had been chasing each other around in ever decreasing circles, a small band of dedicated people had designed and built the internal electrical system. As these people had little knowledge of these things it was a miracle that it worked. At the same time much of the interior of the hut was improved. Water heaters, a shower, a new plumbing system, and a redesigned ladies toilet area were all fitted.

In 1991 Jeff stood down as Hut Warden and Trevor Iceton took over. Trevor quite rightly decided that members had had enough of working on the cottage and so working meets were scaled down to painting and minor maintenance. Trevor's main task was getting everything back onto an operational basis after the traumas of the installation.

Trevor's first major task was the Hermitage roof. It was old and leaking and the hut team decided it should be replaced, in the summer of 1993. Trevor ordered the materials, and on a weekend of glorious weather a small party set to and removed the roof. By the end of the weekend the timbers and felting were in place and left for the following weekend. The following week tiling was started and the inside of the roof timberlined. The tiling was finished by a professional tiler the next week. The whole procedure went without any major problems much to the relief of Trevor, who thought he was going to be left in charge of a hut without a roof.

In 1993 it was decided that the hut should be maintained by a small group so as to ease the burden on the hut warden, Mike Brandrith being co-opted as hut warden and leader of the hut group. This delegation of duties has so far proved very successful. Also in 1993 John France and Jim Pearson were professionally hired to refit the interior of the kitchen, which they did extremely well, fitting new benches, sinks and shelves, dramatically improving the hut as a result. The next major project will be the replacement of the main hut roof. The hut at present seems to be doing very well, being booked up well in advance and making a healthy profit. This is in no small thanks to the many members and friends who have assisted in all the tasks over the years. May the next 50 years be as successful and rewarding.

Walks from the Bowderstone
Hedley Smith

Years ago in conversation with someone in a pub, I was told the NMC were a bunch of elderly ramblers keen on raising points of order at meetings. About a year later, in similar conversation, I was told the NMC were a bunch of hard men who climbed nothing less than HVS (E numbers were scarce in those days). It just goes to show how much rubbish gets spread about and how just a little of the truth seems to go a long way.

I am told that in the 1960's there were several walking meets each year. There were still one or two when I joined in the early 1970's, but since then the Club seems to have mainly concentrated on rock climbing. The only regular walking meet the club has had for many years is the Cheviot Walk on the Saturday of the Ceilidh which, before the licensing laws were changed, used to be a popular event with the young and fit. The object of the exercise was to get over Cheviot, Comb Fell and Hedgehope and down to the cars and back to Wooler before the pubs shut.

It was not until after a superb family holiday at Bowderstone Cottage in 1976, when it never rained for the ten days we were there, that I began to realise the potential of the Cottage as a base for real high class walking. Bowderstone Cottage is situated in the gap between two of the spokes radiating from the hub of the Lake District and is handily situated for crossing over these spokes into adjoining valleys, either directly or after a short drive to Seathwaite. Most of my favourite walks have an adjoining valley as a feature, even though they do take in the odd summit here and there.

What follows is a description of two of my favourite walks, many of which will be fairly self evident, especially to someone who has one of the beautifully shaded one inch OS maps of the district.

One of the first walks I ever did in the Lakes, destroying the place with triple hobs and trikes, was Gable from Seathwaite. I went via the standard route up to Gillercombe, over Green Gable and on via Windy Gap. It was then I first saw Ennerdale was told there was no road up to it. It seemed remote and very romantic to a young lad from the middle of Leeds. Although there must have been the same forestry road as exists today (the trees were growing even then) the feeling of remoteness still affects me every time I visit the valley. One winter's evening, when admiring my map, it dawned on me that Ennerdale is not very far from Seathwaite, if one goes over the top via Grey Knotts or Brandreth and in demonstrating this Lynn Breen was given her first taste of a good day out and probably Jeff has never forgiven me.

Start by driving to Seathwaite and try to find somewhere to park. Follow the path up Sour Milk Gill and aim for the right hand side of Gillercombe Buttress. The direct route gets you in a tangle with the walls and it may be easier to follow the usual climbers approach, but it seems boggier and further. The idea is to go up the easy way down on the north side of the crag, but those who remember when climbing started at Moderate and not at E1, can always enjoy Rabbit's Trod, 770 feet, Moderately Difficult (page 122 in Bentley Beetham's "Borrowdale" 1953 edition) which brings one to the top of the crag. A good downhill walk in a generally westerly direction will land you on the path from Warnscale Bottom to Haystacks. If your navigation is a lot better than mine you might even hit Blackbeck Tarn at first try. Follow the path over Haystacks, down to Scarth Gap and then down into Ennerdale. There is a pleasant spot for lunch where Scarth Beck enters the forest, if you found the top of Haystacks too crowded by Nuclear Electric's photographers making their blatantly cynical adverts. Pass Black Sail Hostel (the best in the Lakes according to my son) and walk along the north bank of the river until you can see Windy Gap high above you. It's a grand place to walk up to at about 6 o'clock on a summer's evening after a good kip in the valley bottom. Of course if it's thick mist and raining then you should have listened to the weather forecast before setting out. From Windy Gap the way back is straight down Aaron Slack and on the Sty Highway to Stockley Bridge. I find the carefully tailored path down the bottom part of the hill a delight to use, and only hope walkers stick to it rather than taking pointless short cuts and adding to the erosion.

A second sample of the goodies on offer is the ascent of Helvellyn. A fine walk, and one for which you will need two maps if you use the 1:25,000 scale. Start straight from the Cottage and walk south down the road in the early morning light. If the sun is high in the sky you either walk a lot faster than I do, or enjoy roaming the fells in the dark. Turn left at the square recess in the wall and head for Watendlath which you will find charming, as, at this hour in the morning, there will be no one else there. Straight up the hill on the east of the village and at the top turn right along the path towards Blea Tarn.

Ullscarf, a rarely visited spot, is to the south and the notorious bog which surrounds it seems to ooze northwards in places as the ground along here can be boggy. Follow the path which swings to the east and descend to Thirlmere. Walk round its southern end and follow the road towards Keswick for about half a mile where you turn right up a clearly marked path which leads eventually to the top of Helvellyn.

Pause a while amongst the assembled hoards, many of whom will have struggled up from Patterdale or Glenridding and now face the arduous descent. At this stage the novice to real walking is advised not to start thinking about how far he or she has to go to get back.

Choose a descent route that takes you as near to the northern end of Thirlmere as possible, as you will have to walk round it. The map indicates you can walk along the side of the reservoir around Great How but I always seem to miss that somehow and walk along the road. Perhaps I should try looking at the map when actually out walking! At the junction of the minor roads to the west of the reservoir turn right for a short way and then left up a steep path to the ancient fort at Castle Crag. Follow the forestry road in a generally southerly direction, along the deer fence, until you are able to get through one of those fancy leaning gates on to the open moor. Head for the highest point, High Seat, which on the metric maps is given a meaningless height of 608 metres. The one inch map is more romantic at 1996 feet, which means your head is again over 2,000 feet.

Wander down the hillside in the general direction of west, the idea being to cross Watendlath Beck by the footbridge which gives access to the path through the woods. Go past Shepherds and onto the Borrowdale road at High Lodore Farm, where you can get tea and ice cream. By now my feet are usually killing me as the old Dachsteins are a bit past their best, but ignoring the swollen ankles, stagger along the road to the Cottage where several well deserved swigs from the bottle of malt you wisely left behind will make you feel well enough for a short walk along the road to the Scafell.

Some Northumbrian Climbing Guides
Norman Haighton

I am always impressed by the celebrities interviewed in the media who seem able to recall every aspect of their long lives in tedious detail. I can barely remember what I had for breakfast.

"Can you write a few words about the old days? You know, the early guides and all that". A piece of cake, until I sit down in front of my PC and realise that I can't remember a thing about it. "I know, I'll browse through the guides, that'll trigger the thoughts". Alas, can't even find a copy. I used to have thousands in the garage. "Try the old photos, they'll bring back the memories". Large box dragged out and an archaeological dig through the strata of time. On top, mountain biking stuff, weddings of nephews and nieces, packaged holidays. Down below it's sail boarding, houses, teenage kids, camping holidays. Keep burrowing (back to the 70s), young kids, babies, no holidays. Then I strike the real stuff; 1965 Julian Alps; 1964 Bregaglia; 1963 Bernese Oberland. Lots of actions shots on Castle Rock, Kilnsey, White Gill, Cloggy. Acres of snow and ice all over Scotland. But where are all the local shots? Had to work hard for these; tucked away in ones and twos between the big stuff. But they brought the memories back!

The Knowe may not mean much to the present generation but it figured heavily in my climbing career. Newly arrived on Tyneside and with no car, a potholer first but prepared to give climbing a try, I took the train to Bardon Mill in late 1961 and walked up towards Crag Lough. Bumped into some rather genteel types near the Knowe and was invited in for tea. During the great snows of 1963 we plodged up through the drifts to stay there (there wasn't much else to do) and I later met my future wife there (an omen if ever there was one).

The 1950 guide was out of print. It was scandalous that no one had produced a new one and the committee discussed the issue frequently with a seriousness only found in committees. The problem seemed to be that various manuscripts had been lying around for long enough but no one wanted to finish the job. So with the brashness of youth I volunteered. My climbing partner was the only other youngster around, Malcolm Lowerson, and he stars in all my photos. He had been living at Warkworth where he had found Jack Rock and soloed several routes. We cleaned up the manuscripts, added what we could and conned the Dalesman into publishing the green, cardboard guide as quickly as possible. It wasn't impressive, or definitive, or a work of art. But it was there, in use on the crags and appreciated.

Most of my early shots are of Crag Lough, on Pinnacle Face, Impossible Buttress or Y Climb. Rope tied to waist, a runner dangling insecurely from a spike every 30 feet or so. But we also ranged wide across the County on Wednesday evenings which was when most of the climbing was done – weekends were for the Lakes. More often than not we soloed all but the most serious. And the countryside looked quite different. Coe Crag was surrounded by open moor; The Belling wasn't submerged under Kielder Water; it all felt more remote without so much intrusion from National Park and Forestry Commission.

The 60s were magic years. Many crags were not written up and there was scope for new, or nearly new, routes all over the place. The team grew steadily – some old hands like Dave Roberts and Hugh Banner and a band of keen youngsters – John Earl, Dennis Lee, Jim Patchett and the like. And gradually the talk turned to the dreaded subject. The new guide. There had to be one and it had to be the best. On reflection that aim isn't usually achieved by doing what we decided to do – produce the guide by committee.

It was an auspicious start. The officially constituted guide book sub-committee got thrown out of the Half Moon in Ryton for noisy behaviour at its first meeting. And we were only discussing grading!

The work was divided up first on the basis of natural ownership. Anyone who had banged on about a particular crag being the bees knees was sent off to do all the routes again and write it all down. It then got down to fingering people for the rest (the list's at the front of the guide). The traditional crags, Crag Lough, Wanney, Simonside took some assigning – a helluva lot of work without much glory. The real sport was had on those crags where a fair bit of climbing had been done but no one had really written it down yet.

If we were going to produce the definitive guide we were going to make sure we had really cracked the main lines. I remember some gripping Wednesday evenings on Ravensheugh and Sandy watching the gurus (particularly Hugh Banner) worming their way up some impossible looking lines. There were superb sunny evenings on Bowden Doors probing unlikely walls; and dark, soggy, lichenous hours on Kyloe in the Wood attempting bulges which ended in vertical pine needle mulch. And what finer end to any climbing day than a few pints in a Northumbrian pub followed by fish and chips in Rothbury or Ponteland.

That was the good side of producing a guide. Climbers are good at climbing and pretty fair at other things like drinking. By and large they aren't very good at joined-up writing. There is some sort of aversion to it and when finally forced into it by frequent editorial badgering, soggy sheets covered with assorted rantings are produced. The editor's task was to convert this into some sort of Standard English. Slowly the material was knocked into shape and typed up by my office typist. Then came the consideration by committee. "He must be bloody joking, that's never Hard VS" and "He must be dreaming, there isn't an overhanging crack on that wall". You know, the usual supportive, constructive comments you get from reviewers of others' work. Mind you, sometimes they were right. The other problem was finding someone to do the illustrations. And then getting them to do them. Dennis Lee did the lion's share as well as doing some of the writing.

We were publishing this guide ourselves. This meant that the Club put up the money and I did the rest. We got the best quote from a printer in Preston so I finally assembled the full set of material and drove it over. Bliss. Nothing to do now but wait and get on with the climbing. Then I discovered the only thing worse than watching golf on television – checking galley proofs. I finally took delivery of 2,000 copies of the guide. They filled most of the spare bedroom.

After that it was plain sailing. Advertise, take orders, deliver invoice, change faulty copies, handle complaints. Discover the mistakes you didn't find in the galleys (it should have been zero G not Xerog). Engage in endless debates about whether such and such a route should have been Very Severe (Mild) or plain Very Severe. Eventually it all died down. It was 1971 and the guide problem was finally solved.

How could we have been so naive. In less than five years a supplement of new routes had to be published. It wasn't just the new guide which stimulated a period of intense crag development. A hard school of climbers was developing which moved standards ever upwards. John Earl and the late Bob Hutchinson were at the centre of this in Northumberland, joined later by Robert and Tommy Smith. I certainly couldn't keep up with it and my interest waned somewhat.

But I clearly couldn't escape yet. There I was in 1977, agreeing to edit and publish yet another guide. There was more of the administration and less of the climbing in it for me this time. We used the same formula – splitting up the work among several people. But this time we could build directly onto the text of the 1971 guide. Checking the galleys got no more exciting but at least the printer's was nearby. And now I had a bigger house with a large garage which could hold all 3,000 copies!

So it came out in 1979 and once I had sold them all (it took until about 1985) I gave up having anything to do with Climbing Guides to Northumberland or to anywhere else. But I don't regret a moment. And I still think that climbing takes some beating. Proper climbing that is, out on the moors and in the mountains, away from it all, clinging onto some crag. I haven't been on a Northumbrian crag for years. But last year Dave Roberts and I were down in Southern France and we decided to have a go at a crag down there. A proper crag on a real mountain – in fact one of the few you can't get up without some genuine rock climbing. We got to the top of Mont Aiguille in three hours from the valley and didn't meet a soul all day (it was midweek and September). I thought it was pretty good for a couple of old'uns.

SIX DECADES OF THE CLUB
Compiled by Stephen Porteus

During the decades since its formation in 1945 to the present, our club has seen many changes. Crags that once required an all day or even full weekend bus meet are now given flying visits on a Wednesday night including a stop at the pub.

The need for a club hut in Northumberland itself long since vanished; the Bowderstone is a delightful asset from the social point of view but hardly as essential to the club's activities as the Knowe or Antic Hay once were. There is sometimes even talk of a hut in the south of France!

Climbing techniques and standards have advanced beyond all recognition helped by improvements in equipment and the ability to train in all weathers in the comfortable environment of the modern climbing wall.

The essays that follow, give an insight into the club in each of the six decades of its existence, yet despite the changes that have occurred during the last 50 years they contain a common thread; enthusiasm for the crags and hills of our fine county and beyond, coupled with that essential quality of any club, good company and as we say good "crack".

The Forties
An Interview with Basil Butcher

How did the formation of the NMC come about?
Frank Oakes-Smith and myself both had cottages near Crag Lough to which up to a dozen or 15 people would come to stay for a weekend, climbing on the crag. King's College Climbing Club members were also climbing on Crag Lough at this time and although there was no rivalry between us, the College climbers were climbing routes which they believed had not previously been done and this was not the case. I suggested to Professor Emrys Williams of King's College that we should establish something more concrete. A meeting was held in Newcastle and the result was the formation of the NMC.

What was the club like in its early days?
The club was very active. The Lake District was popular as were bus meets. After a while a decision was made to concentrate our efforts in the Cheviots. I was friendly with the farmer at Mount Hooley. Parties would sleep in his barn. Eventually we set up a permanent tent to sleep 12, near the stream, which was dammed annually for swimming and washing. It also provided a source of trout.

How did the club come to have Antic Hay and The Knowe?
The club took over the tenancy of Antic Hay at Winshields Farm from myself in 1945. I had been the tenant of Antic Hay since 1939, from where climbing continued on Crag Lough during the war. The later move to the Knowe was simply in order to accommodate more people: sleeping facilities at Antic Hay were in the barn.

What was climbing like in Northumberland in the 1940's?
We mostly climbed in boots or 'rubbers', which were black Woolworth's gym shoes costing 6d a pair.

Our main interest was putting up new climbs. Most of the day would be taken up with gardening routes. As an engineering student I was fortunate enough to be able to make a few karabiners. Most didn't have them, although some equipment was available from Robert Laurie of London. Most people began by using 27s-6d clinker boots from Timpson's.

Was the NMC a success in its early days?
Great interest in the club existed. We were expanding onto new crags all the time. The King's College Club had already produced a guide book to Simonside so there was a lot of interest in climbing new routes. The characters who made the most impact in the early days were those who pioneered new routes: Charlie Gosman, Bob Conn, Brian Cooke, Bill Miller, Tony Moulam and, a little later at Kyloe, Gill Lewis, Eric Clarke and myself. Charlie Gosman always used to pick up the poker from the hearth at Antic Hay for gardening purposes on the crag. Poker Chimney got its name after he spent most of one day cleaning out a route at Crag Lough with his poker and then, unroped, slid all the way to the bottom!

Waiting for the transport, Wanneys Meet, 1945–46. Photograph: Angus McDonald.

The Fifties
Hilda Bath

I suppose my love of the outdoor life stems from my grandfather. A true Victorian, he would leave his wife and three daughters each weekend to go off walking or cycling perhaps a respite from four women in the house!

After school, college and working away I eventually returned to the North East and decided to go on a climbing course organised by the Mountaineering Association. I can't remember how I found out about it! Anyway it was in Langdale – I hired a rope and set forth on public transport onto the unknown! Having enjoyed the course so much, I did another two – one in the Lakes, the other in North Wales. I was even awarded certificates!

Then I had a weekend in Ennerdale (October 1957) with friends who belonged to the Cleveland MC – all very good climbers – I just had to do my limited best! They knew the name of the NMC secretary, passed it on to me and so my relationship with the Club began, which gave me so many happy memories and good friends.

The first meet I attended was on the 27 April 1957 at Simonside which was a "Beginners' Meet". It does not seem 37 years ago. At that time, the only hut the Club had was the Knowe. Most of my memories seem tied up with working meets! The water supply was almost non existent and the other facilities included the "Cabin in the Sky". For club meets we ventured further afield – the Lakes and Scotland – using other club huts.

At last we decided to try to find a hut of our own in the Lakes and as a Committee we visited many places until we eventually found the Bowderstone. At first sight it was boarded up and very depressing. We managed to lease it from the National Trust and set to work to improve it.

Nev Hannaby at Bowden Doors in 1958, leading The Corner, HVS, 5a. Note the jammed knots for protection.

Our first New Year was celebrated in style – before midnight we all trooped up the ladder armed with drinks, torches and a radio – so we saw in the New Year on the top of the Bowderstone itself. The large room had no bunks at all then – just large piles of timber waiting to be used – the first and last time I've slept on a large pile of wood stacked in a corner. There was much work to be done but gradually it was completed. In between the working meets were normal meets and Annual Dinners usually held at the Royal Oak in Keswick.

I have many other memories – the Annual "bus meet" not forgetting the one in 1959 when we were overtaken by very bad weather and "lost" two members. We even made the headlines in the "Newcastle Journal" and "Evening Chronicle"! If you're wondering how I remembered dates, blame it on my grandfather. He worked for the "Sunderland Echo" and I've always kept journals.

The Sixties
Norman E Haighton

As in every club at every period there were old'uns and young'uns. I was then in the latter category. The old'uns ran the club, arranged meets and dinners, tended to prefer walking to climbing, were also in the FRCC and generally took exception to the young'uns.

Transport was a big problem. Few had cars so buses were often hired. The latter had advantages – get dropped off in Alwinton and picked up in Yetholm. Roads were poor but it didn't stop us going to Scotland pretty often, especially in winter. Arriving in the early hours to camp in Glen Nevis or Glencoe, getting back just before work on Monday morning. Mac had a firm's van (advertising Players Navy Cut) which carried such as Gordon Mitchell, John Porter, Malcolm 3Ts and Mike Saunders on these events. Then John Pentland and I both bought GLVs (A35s – grand little vans) and there was no stopping us. Took them to the Alps in Convoy in 1964. Having ridden pillion to the Alps in 1963 the GLV was a great luxury.

The only Northumbrian crags which got must attention at first were The Wanney's, Simonside and Crag Lough. We stayed often at the Knowe and climbed on the Whin Sill. There were major social events involving a walk across the fields to the Twice Brewed with a barrel waiting at the Knowe for our return. Riotous behaviour involving a tree trunk led to rustication's on one occasion. Later we turned to other crags. Surprisingly it wasn't Bowden Doors or Kyloe but, with hindsight, a bizarre collection including Causey Quarry, Crag Point, Coe and Cullernose (there's a frightener for you – vertical Whin Sill with guano and tide to contend with). I can only assume that the letter C was in vogue.

But the Lakes was our favourite venue. We camped at Rosthwaite or Wasdale Head and climbed on Castle Rock, Scafell and White Gill using the old, fawn FRCC guides. The weather was just as bad then and the pub was for drying the outside as well as wetting the inside.

I still have contact with many of the group I climbed with then. Many of them still get out on the hills. The NMC was good training.

The Seventies
Stephen Porteus

Great Wanney on a wet, windy January day is a far cry from the cosseting environment of the Berghaus Wall enjoyed by the novices of today; climbing walls hadn't been invented then. I had gone there with Ian Henderson who had recently left school with a sound knowledge of the basics of ropework and so on, which he patiently passed on to me. The Wanneys were the favourite venue for one very good reason; the crag was nearer to home than anywhere else and a pound would buy the couple of gallons needed to get us there and back and even a pint on the way home.

After several visits we were just gaining confidence on the easier Diffs when we met with some climbers of obvious experience who were cruising nonchalantly up Main Wall, which at that time was the pinnacle of our ambitions. Out of pity for our incompetence they suggested that we should consider joining their club, the NMC. It subsequently transpired that they were members of considerable standing, Gordon Mitchell, Graham Townsend and Geoff Jackson, the then President.

It was some months later when we decided to venture out on a Club meet, at Simonside and Ravensheugh. Conditions were claggy and clarty and not a bit suitable for impressing the dignitaries present. There were one or two other prospective members including one fit looking, young(ish) chap, John Earl. After some slithering and sliding on Simonside we marched to Ravehsheugh which was even wetter. Not a lot was done except standing about until the said John Earl stylishly soloed an awkward little route which we now know as Mole. We made as if to follow him but were informed, gently but firmly by the Meet Leader that John was a very good climber. This left us in no doubt as to the impression we had made.

Gradually, confidence on the rock increased and the dizzy heights of the Severe grade and Club membership were attained. In those days election to membership was a hard pitch to climb but all the more satisfying for that.

Weekend meets became habit forming and many memorable trips to the Lakes and Scotland resulted; fine climbs, dry rock, constantly excellent weather, perfect winter ice, Hartleys XB in flawless condition and sometimes collected from the pub in Dave Roberts' purpose designed beer bucket for consumption on the campsite during impromptu cricket matches.

Wednesday evenings became an essential part of the week; winter in The Bridge Hotel and in summer on the crags. Superb warm nights at Bowden Doors, Ravensheugh, Crag Lough. The lack of real beer in the hostelries of the county made lengthy drives from crag to pub essential. The heated debate in the pub about the following week's venue was always a high point of the night with David Cox presiding as an unofficial arbitrator; this was long before the days of the Wednesday venues being debated by the Committee, listed in the Club circular (and resolutely ignored by the majority). The only sop to organisation was the appointment of a Wednesday evening co-ordinator whose role was to make life easier for prospective members and those in need of transport. This was to be my undoing; I was asked to take on this job in 1977 and received a call from the same John Earl who by then was Club Secretary. Would I look after a female prospective member, Hilary Charlton, who needed a lift to the crag. I agreed, somewhat reluctantly, and the rest, as they say, is history.

The Eighties
Cliff Robson

It's nearly midnight. Midwinter. The Clachaig Inn Glencoe in the late 80s … Somewhere in the darkness murky figures struggle to hammer tent pegs into frozen ground. Next morning before it's barely light they are on their way to claim a route in the Lost Valley. Weary but high on achievement they return, cook a meal and fall into the Clachaig to plan how to do it all again the next day. After innumerable pints, probably stretching into double figures, they crawl back into icy tents and pray for good weather. The traditional fish and chip stop at Calendar or Pathhead is the highlight of the long journey home to become an ordinary working person on Monday morning.

I had been to the Alps a couple of times and now I wanted to extend my expertise on snow and ice. That's how I discovered the NMC. Robin and Barbara Sillem lent me a tent with a porous ground sheet and it all happened. There was ice. There was snow. There were, it seems, countless weekends heading out of a gloomy Tyneside Friday evening rush hour to a weekend of adventure, ale and achievement. Perhaps it was the golden age of NMC winter meets. One Easter weekend in Aviemore an amazing 15 or 20 people arrived for one NMC meet, to camp in sub-zero temperatures for several days of brilliant route bagging in the Cairngorms. But then the snow vanished, the ice stopped appearing and Scottish winter meets turned into weekend trips to Nevis Sports.

Then there was rock climbing. I hadn't joined to rock climb but to mountaineer. The rock climbing was something to develop my rope work between Easter and the start of the Alpine climbing season. I scanned the list of Wednesday evening meets. Coe Crag sounded promising. A slight drizzle began to fall as I headed up into the woods following rather vague directions. Half an hour later the drizzle had turned to rain as I now know it always does on Coe Crag meets. I had reached open ground but still no crag. I wandered in a state of forlorn hope past the misty shape of a buttress. "Want the end of a rope for this route?" A member! A member's voice! I was almost too ecstatic to talk. Rain bounced off my helmet and soaked my Super Rats as I was hauled up Raven's Buttress. And in the Linden Hall pub it all became worthwhile. I was a member swapping yarns with other members. So it was on many a subsequent meet. I would stumble my way towards a frequently rain sodden crag in the middle of Northumberland with only a Whillans and a pair of Super Rats to my name and each time as I was about to despair the friendly voice of a member would toss me an end of rope. Thanks Tony!

The final jigsaw piece of my recollections of those halcyon days was of course the winter social programme. It's difficult to imagine what winter Wednesdays evenings were like before I discovered NMC winter socials. In a room resembling the long abandoned residence of an alcoholic furniture remover with a passionate grudge against DIY, a seductive potion of travellers' tales and exotic slides fuelled the badinage and camaraderie only produced by climbers over jars of the amber nectar.

Outside the canny folk of Benton went about their ordinary lives but in that hallowed room above the Brandling in South Gosforth, in the shadow of the Chinese take away and a stone's throw from South Gosforth Fisheries, I was transfixed. Inspiration! That's what it was. And it was here that future adventures were conceived, planned and maybe eventually executed. Anything was possible. Absolutely anything!

The Nineties
Christine Johnston

My first impressions of the Northumbrian Mountaineering Club are remembered in snatches, clouded by memories of more recent meets, moves, climbs and falls.

There are two clear memories that come from a time before I joined the club. The first is that friends and climbing associates kept warning me about the NMC, saying that they were unfriendly and unwelcoming to anybody who did not climb at least E3. The second was climbing in Northumberland, probably at Bowden Doors, and seeing these quiet, bemuscled, lycra clad men climbing on what looked to me, in my naivety, smooth rock and using, successfully, grains of sand for holds. At this point I decided the NMC was not for me. For one thing I am rarely described as quiet, especially when climbing, and secondly I can not levitate.

It was a small piece of paper on the wall at Wild Trak that made me take the first steps to joining. "Women wanted". This is just the sort of phrase which normally has me reaching for my soap box and delivering a loud, lengthy monologue. I went inside to have a word with the manager; he kindly loaned me a pen and I took note of the telephone number on the bottom of the notice.

I will never forget my first meet, one of the Wednesday night meets at Kyloe, or was it Bowden? My car exhaust fell off. There I was with a car full of strangers, just past Alnwick, and the silencer bouncing off the road, but everybody being too polite to mention that the funny scraping and banging noises were coming from the back of my car. Luckily I had all my climbing gear with me. One of my not so short extenders and a krab soon solved the problem.

It was Kyloe. As we walked through the undergrowth we passed what looked to me to be very reasonable, but empty rock, not a soul to be seen. Not a very promising start. Then we walked out of the mile high ferns into a darkened area, where the rock was covered in people, not only climbing, but climbing rock with holds and speaking while they did it. Things were looking up. After seconding a severe I decided to lead a starred Hard Severe. The then president looked at me with great concern. "Be careful, it's hard," was his warning. So with great care I went up the HS. It was wonderful. I pointed out that I did not think that it was undergraded. His response was, "I always find climbs with 'hard' in their grade difficult". What more could I say? When the climbing was complete everybody went off to the pub, where they sold real beer. Pity I was driving, but I knew then that this was a club I would grow to like.

After many successful Wednesday evenings I went on a weekend meet, a barbecue at the Bowderstone Hut. The three days have left me with many mixed and jumbled memories: knuckle in crack, pain, relief, food, sausages, fire light, beer, chat, rugby, friends, lonely, sausages, new classic, second pitch, dark, long walk, dry pub!, sausages, ill, hammock, Ardus, good weekend.

Looking back at those days before I joined the NMC, with much more experience, I smile at my thoughts of the climbers at Bowden Doors and realise that the holds they were using would cause even a slug with super glue to have problems. After my initial fears and mishaps I have grown to enjoy the enthusiasm for climbing and beer that the members of the NMC display, and think what I would have missed if I had listened to obsolete advice.

On the Snow Peak
(Check this one Baudelaire)
Bob Hutchinson

I fear the monstrous hand
That once clawed out this ranged distance
And sculptured out a gigantic scene of torment
Of bristling tortured limbs and twisted muscles
Forever knit beneath snows ghastly marble;
And yet I am at peace here
High above the silent valleys and sleeping lakes
While wind blows softly and sun lights the snows
And white flame peaks soar high as angels
Dreaming, dreaming, in the ice blue depths of heaven

The Wind, Hedgehope Hill, January 1993
Martin Cooper

Blasted and beaten by the pummelling blast,
Across wind swept, desolate moorland waste,
Staggering slowly upwards
Grasping for fence posts and gasping for breath,
I reached the summit.

Far above, clouds scud across the darkening sky
Glimpses of Cheviot, barren and bleak to the North,
Wasteland, frequented by grouse, the occasional sheep and vain,
Demented walkers such as I.

Eastwards a faint line marks the coast, islands beyond
In summer day-tripping sun seekers people the beaches there.
Today the elements will lift sand and hurl it, mockingly, seawards,
Throw such seabirds as dare to rise upwards from dune or rock
Across the wind torn sky, showing the futility of
Any effort to fly in the face of this gale.
Hurriedly I sip coffee, pull my hood still tighter round my face
And set off once more into the biting blast.

Saturday's Widow
Joan Murley

"I'll just get up now to get my things together", he whispers as he leans over and gives me a gentle peck before jumping out of bed. "I'll not make any noise."

I open one eye to look at the clock 5.45 am! Both bedroom lights are on, landing light, bathroom light and the whistling begins.

"Colin – LIGHTS."

"Oops," he says as he comes back in and turns them off.

"Sorry, I'll bring you a cup of tea later."

THEN the shuffling and rummaging begins. The ceremonial packing of the rucksack; quick draws, karabiners, nuts friends and ropes all fondled and caressed with thoughts of the day ahead.

"Where is it? Where is it? Joan have you seen my crag mat? Did you wash it?"

"No, I put it in a bucket, which you'll find behind the laundry basket in the bathroom."

"Oh crikey, I'll wash it now", he says, "and put the heating on, so it will dry on the radiator".

After the third drawer had been opened and shut, I finally ask him what it is he is looking for?

"My purple top with the climber on, I thought would go best with these tights."

I squint at the garish rainbow spectrum of colours in the tights brandished before me. Well, never mind, I'm sure the crag will be well out of sight. Crash, bang, thump as he makes his way across to the wardrobe shelf, falling over the wood which is part of the unfinished dressing table.

"I'll get a bit of that done when I get home tonight." he says.

"Will you be home early enough?"

"I've found my top." He pulls it from the shelf and swiftly disappears around the bedroom door. Six thumps down the stairs, then six thumps back to turn bedroom light out before descending stairs to begin next stage of the Saturday morning ritual.

One, two, three and now the rhythmic beat of "Gonna Live On Solid Rock'" begins to vibrate from the floor boards.

Good morning – Dire Straits. I ring down to remind him Danny and Hazel next door don't need to be up.

"Oops, sorry, right I'll just finish making my sandwiches and flask and I'll bring you that cup of tea, seeing as you are awake."

I pull the pillows over my head and snuggle down, knowing it's best to stay in bed whilst he is making his finishing touches. I think Colin's epitaph will be "Oops sorry." I begin to drift into sleep.

Suddenly the weight of Colin lands on my feet. "Oops sorry, here's your tea. I think I'll have another go at Fifty for Five today," he says, pushing a well thumbed picture from "Extreme Rock" at me.

"Oh crikey is that the time – haven't rung yet to see if it's John's or Bob's we're meeting at. Bye love ."

In the kitchen Colin has left his mark. There's a ring on the bench showing where the flask stood with coffee and sugar granules around the circle. Half a loaf of bread remains with crumbs from board to floor. I open the blind and see what a rotten day it is. Yes I think they will be back early when it's chucking down so hard.

… MUCH LATER. Now if he comes straight into the bedroom that means they have travelled far to find a dry spot. If he goes into loo first that means it has been a long session in pub. Oh well – loo first. I lie spread over the bed fast asleep, as seen in movies.

"Are you awake? I've had a great day."

"Uh, what time is it?" I stretch and look at clock. "What time is it?" I repeat, it's best to get him to actually say the time to provoke feelings of guilt and ensure the grass will get cut tomorrow. (Cutting the grass will let him think he is clocking up 'brownie points').

"It's 20 to 12." He puts his arm around me from which I immediately recoil, as the Eau de Escalade reaches my nose, BO (normal), damp vegetation (Kyloe in the Wood), stale beer and smoke (Millstone).

"Where have you managed to climb in this rain?"

"We found a brilliant overhang, didn't notice the rain." He then begins to give a blow by blow account of each move and each clip made. Fastly resembling an Indian Chief during a war dance as arms and legs flail in every direction.

"I'll make a coffee." I struggle into my dressing gown and follow him downstairs as he begins a long monologue about what he will do next week to make sure he bags the route … this time. My thoughts are of leopards and spots, old dogs and new tricks!

Working Class
Peter Kirton

The mid 1980s were particularly fruitful years for the club's newsletter. The publication of one or two outstanding articles seemed to provoke others and, for a year or two, the newsletter became more than just a vehicle for meet reports and information. Pete Kirton was undoubtedly the most prolific and the most talented contributor at the time. Indeed, for a short while, he even had his own column. Working Class, a classic of its kind, was originally published under the assumed name, D Johnson. There is no doubt, however, that it was a product of the Kirton pen. The question of who was, in fact, the editor of the newsletter at this time is a subject still hotly disputed.

Working Class was a 20 foot gauntlet of flat black adamantine sandstone, gracing the more manly, northern end of Bowden Doors. Leaning slightly towards the Cheviot Hills and tendonitis it was a blatant unshirkable challenge, striking Robert Smith and myself all the more painfully because of its tantalising almost possibility. So it was nothing more than a presumptuous name and a mutual aim, the only thing we did share apart from thermos flasks and spectacularly rococo legs. Blonde moustachioed guru versus unsightly stooge we bouldered, bitched and competed with each other over three Northumbrian winters and Working Class offered a tough battleground for our wildly differing climbing styles.

Smith was gnarlier than me by almost ten years, a decade of hard uncomfortable graft keeping other people warm and amorous by felting the roofs of Tyneside. Arriving at Bowden Doors like a case history from a Sociology text, on day release from a distant world of Embassy No. 6, pub dominoes, bent deals and straight sex, he would roll up his sweater sleeve to boast, crowning cliché, a tattooed forearm. But bickering our way leftwards along the crag, bouldering at half throttle to save skin, energy and ego for the Class, he displayed a spontaneous fluid dynamism breezily divorced from monotonous toil, with a grace and timing I have never witnessed the equal of. He had already capitalised on this aerial talent by greedily sandwiching Working Class between sister problems Toffs and Poverty. Both demanded crux jumps off the ground, so as climbs they were unique; once settled on the rock you gained a valid tick. Which I never did. Poverty ('because there's nowt there') was Smith's showpiece, and so specialist it must have been personally tailored. Starting by standing diagonally left of the problem, he sprinted aggressively towards it then, time for bed, boing, snatched at poor holds and frantically clamped on. All he missed was Margot Fonteyn.

Fortunately for me, Working Class itself promised to be far less effete, no place for Morris Dancing. Fortunately, because although Smith's adolescent biceps were passably masculine, disparately weak fingers condemned him to history, not mythology. All that balletic finesse throttled by his own dud tips, then trampled upon by my brutish storm-trooping rock attack. Beauty and The Beast, our similar reach and span sharpened a fine dichotomy by ensuring that we fought on a symmetrical court. My only other weapon was an outspoken cultivated arrogance. Knowledge acquired by much obsequious toadying to the country's top climbers had impressed upon me the importance of a well nurtured ego in sapping ones opponent's confidence. With practice, to catatonia.

No Nobler County

Old and past it, eh Kirton?

Chalk your way out of that then!

The blistered and creased upper part of the Class was weeny riddled, so the problem was reaching the first crease at 12 feet. A rounded ear-shaped layaway gained at a stretch from the ground was the sole employable hold in that slippery pre-resin era. Well, confronted by overhanging slopeys Smith reacted like a nun in a kipper shed, so moving and thinking laterally he concocted a bizarre and subtle solution begging a sort of off-beat pansy dynamic. After the initial southpaw crank onto the wall he crouched sideways and then he stood up on nothing in an attempt to grab the crease with his left hand. This rash dismissal of the only decent hold was compounded by the move's off-balance nature, forcing a token pirouette out and away from the wall, not so much hitting the crease as waving it a dizzy farewell. My own prosaic answer was of course the antithesis of Smith's febrile choreography. A savage full frontal layback linking the ear to the crease was my over ambitious intention, shot down by screaming fingers and overawed overrated arms.

By Christmas 84 I had quit climbing, a two month bender precipitating long term admission to St Nick's on diagnosis of bipolar syndrome. Phil Davidson hit the County the week following my hospitalisation in Spring 85, and managed a three fall rockover on lousy holds, stabbing us with a contemptuous and shaming 6b grade. This kicked the old man back into his second childhood and success on the dynamic one Wednesday evening in June. A ward orderly told me all this with solicitous but needless regard for my condition. After all, nobody likes to see Nastase beaten by Roscoe Tanner. And besides, the food's very nice in here.

Simonside, midsummer sunset. Photograph: Andy Birtwistle.

Grundy's Knowe, with period transport. Photograph: Derek Craggs.

*The Bowderstone, Borrowdale.
Painting by Atkinson Grimshaw, 1864.*

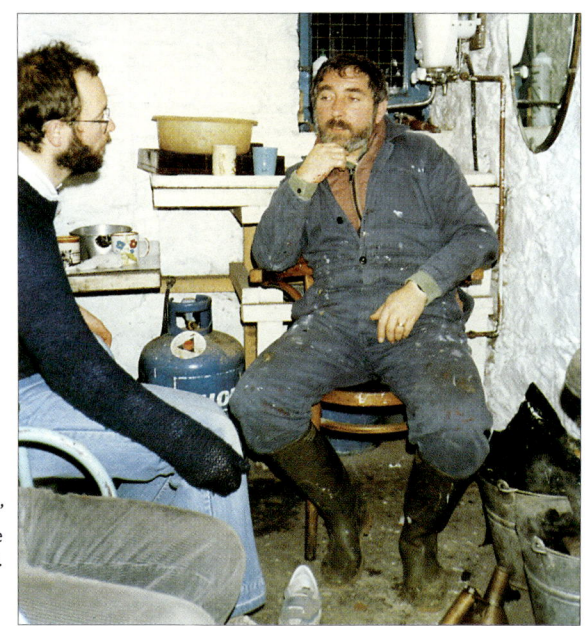

*"Look at it this way, my son."
Tom Hammill hands over the
hut wardenship to Jeff Breen.*

Wednesday night at the crag – Ravensheugh 1980s. Photograph: Steve Crowe.

"Where once was beach" – Simonside. Photograph: Chris Davis.

Colin Murley on Thunder Crack, Simonside. Photograph: Andy Birtwistle.

Walking out from Henhole.
Photograph: Rick Barnes.

A classic of The County. Andy Birtwistle on Marcher Lord, Berryhill Crag. Photograph: Andy Birtwistle collection.

*Dave Cuthbertson bouldering at
Back Bowden Doors, 1994.
Photograph: D Cuthbertson Collection.*

*Bouldering at Bowden Doors,
Tommy Smith on Transformer.
Photograph: Andy Birtwistle.*

Thin, VS, 5a. The Belling.
Climber: Ed Williams.
The lower half now
requires sub-aqua gear.
Photograph: Andy Birtwistle.

Bob Smith taking a step into the future, November 1987 – the first ascent of On the Rocks, E6, 6c, Back Bowden Doors. Photograph: Andy Birtwistle.

*Northumberland's best ice climb.
Alan Hinkes on the Bizzle Burn.
Photograph: Steve Crowe.*

The next generation. Andrew Earl on the first ascent of Bones Don't Bounce, E5, 6C, at Whiteheugh Crag. Photograph: Steve Crowe.

Karin Magog bouldering at Rothley Boulders.
Photograph: Steve Crowe.

The Secluded County.
Climber: Andy Moss.
Photographer: Andy Birtwistle.

Rick Barnes on Pinnacle Face, Crag Lough – NMC 50th Anniversary Meet. Photograph: Andy Birtwistle.

NMC 50th anniversary meet,
Crag Lough, 23rd June 1995.
Photograph: Andy Birtwistle.

Northumberland Rock

January 1995, Andrew Earl on the pockets traverse, Back Bowden Doors. Photograph: John Earl.

Bob Hutchinson and John Earl after the first ascent of The Butcher, Jack Rock. Photograph: John Earl Collection.

Northumbrian Exertions
H Keith Gregory

My first contact with Northumberland rock came through friendship with a Bensham family in the late 1930s. I worked with Bill Farnsworth whose brother Harry was a keen cyclist and time trialist. Bill and I were based near Manors as telephone technicians on the Newcastle outer section. Just before war was declared the Farnsworths got me to join them on a bike tour of Scotland. On my heavy BSA keeping them in sight was not always possible, but even after a day's hard work, never having seen such fine hill-country before, I usually ended with a solo walk in the evenings, cycling shoes notwithstanding. Within a few days I decided that when back in Newcastle alternative kit would be needed.

The boots, including the clinkers, were bought from Timpsons for not much over a pound – then best bitter was less than three (present) pence a pint – and they were soon very comfortable, after local walks and Mars oil. In March 1940 I changed buses at Carlisle, got off the second at Shap and walked westwards. Using youth hostels, the Trevelyans being in my thoughts, I turned back after Wasdale, zigzagged to Honister and over the Derwent Fells to get back via Keswick. Towards the end of 1940 I began to meet other fell-walkers.

The first I met was Edward Emley who had wide knowledge of Northumbrian walks and climbs and ideas about Scotland, where we arranged to go for two weeks. We traversed 20 or more tops from Ben More and Stob Binnein, all of Cruachan – had a longish slide on frozen snow coming off the west end – both flanks of Glen Coe and all the Mamores. Finally from our Fort William bed and breakfast a walk up the Ben and down to catch the two-forty train back to Newcastle.

Before going to Scotland we had had a trial run in the College Valley staying with the Cowans at Mounthooley. We did short climbs near at hand then, next day, went up into Henhole and did several climbs including two longer ones, even though by then the weather and rock were very wet. On Northumbrian rock at last! This so impressed me that I retain only fragmented and uncertain memories – very wet, black rock; vegetation; awkward angles – mostly steep and, in a corner, an enormous nest of twigs with the most awful pong.

The second group of companions I met each Wednesday evening in the cafe above the news cinema in Pilgrim Street, a group of fellwalkers and climbers. There plans were made for the next weekend foray, normally a long walk, sometimes including a crag. Usual shelter would be a youth hostel, tent or a barn, or later at Antic Hay – a small room and a half at the end of one of Dick Green's beast sheds at Winshields farm near Once Brewed, rented at that time by Pat Allinson. Those plans were often modified or abandoned because, with war now in it's second year, disruptions, shortages and other abnormalities had ensued. Friends left for the armed or other services: of those who remained most would work on a Saturday morning and for some even a seven day working week had to be accepted. In other words, in that period between 1940 and 1945 opportunities for climbing were lost simply through restrictions on moving from A to B and on free time or undisturbed sleep or clothing and equipment.

An example will be useful. Why was the College Valley so important to us at that time? Well, most of you will know what superb walking country can be reached from a base near its head. There were still buses from Newcastle to Wooler. It was a fair walk and to reach Mounthooley on Saturday night was relief indeed because here were basic comforts in abundance: warmth from the peats to go with the oil lamps, lots of good farm food, good crack with Dan and Mabel, then the soft sounds of sheep, beast and burn nearby; no planes nor air raid sirens and a good day ahead.

There was too, certainly for most of us, a further restriction: information. No climbing guides and no knowledge whence information could be had. So we went with light loads to walk if hitches failed to a small number of locations where, by word of mouth, were known to be crags on which climbs existed. These included The Wanneys, Simonside, Crag Lough and the College Valley and at each we knew of only a few named routes. Do you now recognize such names as Boundary Corner, Troup de Canon, Trapezium Buttress and am I, 50 years since I last climbed in Northumberland, correct in thinking that they have all by now been almost climbed out and that Boundary Corner is likely to be submerged amongst many other climbs, all measured and neatly graded.

At that time the named climbs tended to be those that followed natural lines and which showed that nailed boots had been ahead of you. Where marks went you could follow and where gardening was apparent you felt a degree of assurance. With no marks we just looked for attractive lines and if we were lucky, followed them to a finish. I do not remember any degree of competition to do new routes and any that emerged were simply as a result of experiment. Because of the war most of us had no ready means of recording or telling of a success.

Apart from Edward Emley my regular companion during 1941–43 was Basil Butcher and we did many climbs in the home county and in the Lakes, most of them quickly, on a leading through basis. In the Lakes I eschewed VS routes and I always kept brief notes. For instance, "B route, Gimmer, 29/9/41, BAB, fair conditions, rubbers, no difficult". On that climb we two were the first rope; following us was another embracing at least one ex-president of the Fell and Rock, this subsequent to my application for membership. Expected to lead Amen Corner I was absolutely opposed – as mutterings behind me suggested – to attempting a layback which I have always felt absorbs too much energy and so I got up otherwise. Speaker said, rather acidly, that he had never before observed such a method: Basil being tall, and on that occasion, orthodox, brought forth no comment. Two months later I was accepted as a life member and have ever been in the club's debt: it is, however conditionally, in my will. At that time Basil may have been rather hard up as he joined later and, as you may not know, was in the mid-80s a vice-president.

Probably the first ascent of Main Wall, Crag Lough. Climbers: Basil Butcher and Keith Gregory.

In Northumberland there were others too but I fail with their names. One photograph shows what was our first ascent of Main Wall at Crag Lough. That day was fine, sun at times, rather windy and a group of us were lying around on the path at the top of the crags. After a while I left the group and went down near Trapezium and then worked my way slowly along the foot of the rocks, going East, looking for new lines. A steep wall with an edge to its right looked tempting and I was able, in rubbers, to work up wall and edge for 30 feet or so. One good hold was loose in a socket and could be pushed in and out, effective for both hand and foot. Beyond that holds looked scarce so I climbed down and went to get a rope. The wall at that point seemed to be about 80 feet.

Up on top of the sill the group remained lying in sunshine. Basil came back with me and we managed a good route for those crags, clean and steep, two or three moves rather a stretch, and certainly one of the longest. There was no sign of previous passage and we regarded it as a first ascent but when I wrote the article, "Climbing in Northumberland" for the Fell and Rock Journal of 1946 it was not specifically claimed as such. Indeed, later in that article I wrote that I did not think it much mattered who first did any of the climbs in Northumberland so long as they became better known.

The next issue of the journal for 1947 included a letter to the editor from Winthrop Young in which he wrote, "The author has omitted to verify his history, as to the crags, or to consult earlier numbers of climbing journals" and he went on to give a fair amount of information himself. Young was correct: the article had been done from memory. Indeed, its second sentence was, "Here and now I have neither notes nor maps only memories". However, to have the article noted as pleasant gave me some satisfaction because over many years, Young had justifiably established a high reputation based on his varied abilities and qualities. As a climbing historian he was outstanding and his books based on a wide experience in the Alps and of many locations in Great Britain were widely read. Sad that his foreword to the 1950 NMC guide was not longer.

In 1943 my request for a transfer from Newcastle had been met and I spent the next five years in Whitehaven and Carlisle, exchanging Northumberland for quicker access to higher hills, longer climbs and spells of wetter weather. Transfer to Bristol in 1948 brought more pay but greater distance from proper hills.

Since then I have remained in Somerset or Wiltshire till now, except for a short period back in Tyne and Wear and ten years in Nigeria, where I got to within a few hundred metres of the top of Mount Cameroon. Following retirement in 1981 I have rebuilt a small house in France, an hour's drive from Verdon. Perhaps soon, we may leave the rounded downs of Wiltshire to find a base in which to live near the confluent Tynes. That would mean a longer drive to the Creuse but at least I could perhaps ask two or three adept NMC members to supervise my ascent of Main Wall one fine summer's day.

Reflections
John Earl

This is not intended to be a history of rock climbing in Northumberland, but is my personal recollection of how I have seen its development as a member of the Northumbrian Mountaineering Club over the last 25 years reflected in the crags of Kyloe and Bowden.

I do not want to give the impression that these are the only good crags. As any of you who have climbed in the County know we have a wealth of excellent crags with routes on them every bit as good, and in some cases even better, than the ones mentioned here. However, Kyloe and Bowden have been the forcing ground for standards over this period by both local and raider alike.

I first made contact with the NMC at the time they were preparing the 1971 guide. Ken MacDonald assisted by myself, Ian Cranston and one or two other friends had developed Corby's Crag and following a meeting in a smoke filled back room at the Spit and Vomit (Victoria and Comet) with Norman Haighton and Hugh Banner, were able to persuade them to include it in the forthcoming guide.

Ken, Ian and I went out once or twice with club members. One such visit was to Kyloe in the Wood which at that time was still on the secret list. Kyloe in the Wood was even better then than it is now, although with fitness levels somewhat lower, ascents of the steep pocketed walls were still some way off. Northumberland at this time was about 10 years behind areas like Yorkshire and the Peak District, particularly in respect of jamming. Hugh who excelled at crack climbing must have thought he was in paradise when he arrived in Northumberland and discovered all the unclimbed overhanging cracks. He did the first ascent of Crucifix, slowly climbing the steep wall at the bottom and then swarming up the overhanging crack to the top. Myself and possibly Ken seconded the route encouraged by him telling us that the difficulties were over once the crack was reached, which of course they weren't.

The setting in the woods at this time was superb; there were no self seeders and the crag was topped by large trees which formed an impenetrable canopy. In later years substantial felling took place which reduced the problem of condensation in summer but did not keep the crag as sheltered in winter. The forest floor beneath the crag was thick with pine needles which cushioned the landing superbly.

Ian and I subsequently made enquiries about joining the club and my first "proper" trip out was on the 19th March 1972 with Hugh Banner, Dennis Lee, Mick Foggin, Dave Ladkin, George Micheson, Bob Hutchinson and a couple of other lads. We visited Bowden Doors and had an excellent days climbing, dry, warm and sunny (it always was wasn't it). In those days it had luxuriant grass at it's foot, no top roping grooves at it's top and no chalk on it's holds. We climbed until dusk and then returned to the cars in two groups. I was with Hugh so naturally we left the crag last. Unfortunately when we arrived at his Capri 3000 it wouldn't start. We had driven through fog on our way to the crag and Hugh had not switched his headlights off. This resulted in me arriving home at 2 am the following morning, which was something my new wife was not used to. She quickly discovered, however, that climbing with Hugh inevitably meant epics.

At this time there were, as there are in many clubs, a number of factions which the president of the time, Geoff Jackson, managed to unify to assist Norman Haighton with the production of the 1971 guide. Once produced, however, the reason for the unified approach had gone and these various groups went their separate ways. Hugh was keen to establish a group of enthusiastic young climbers within the club. I more or less fell within this description at the time.

Around the time that Ian and I joined the NMC a sixth former, George Micheson, and a young school teacher, Bob Hutchinson, also joined. Neither had been climbing long and could best be described as talented novices. Ian and I climbed with George for a year or two before he went off to Manchester University, where he gave up what could have been an excellent climbing career for scuba diving. At this time Bob did not come out regularly with our group which comprised of Hugh, Dave Ladkin, Mick Foggin, Dennis Lee, Ian and myself. He was extremely competitive and would make the odd appearance and then go off training like mad for a few weeks.

In the Autumn of 1972 Bob Hutchinson was still lacking in experience, but he was extremely talented, strong and very competitive when he made his first ascent of The Trial which was to be the start of his exceptional new routing achievements in the County and the Lake District which continued until his untimely death in 1978.

Following a week's chance holiday in the Lakes and Derbyshire Bob and I struck up a partnership and climbed and trained together through the winter of 1972. This was before the advent of climbing walls and summer fitness would be substantially lost over the winter months. In an attempt to overcome this, we started visiting the Viaduct and Causey Quarry on mid-week winter evenings, climbing by the light of a Tilley lamp. Needless to say this was highly secretive.

Around this time, as well as winter bouldering in the County (no points awarded if you did not top out), we would regularly visit the gritstone edges of Yorkshire and Derbyshire, perfecting our jamming techniques and mangling our hands. An early reward however was the first free ascent of Overhanging Crack at Bowden Doors, by myself and Bob Hutchinson. It had previously had a chockstone near the top which was threaded to provide a runner and a point of aid for John Hiron before we freed it.

Back Bowden Doors was another crag ripe for development. Alan Austin and Rod Valentine had climbed the roofs to give the aptly named Sorcerer and Sorcerer's Apprentice. These were the test pieces of the time, which not many outside of our group seemed able to climb. In 1975 the Enchanter was the first route to breech the wall between The Witch (climbed the year before by Malcolm Rowe) and Bottle Crack. This was prior to camming devices. However, the good landing justified Bob Hutchinson's leading of it with no protection. The Tube a few years later was a different proposition and at the time the gear seemed minimal and the route serious. I seconded Bob on the first ascent and found it quite steady – not too strenuous with good footholds and rests on the traverse. However when I came to lead it shortly afterwards, it seemed altogether different. The footholds did not feel quite as large and I seemed to be permanently locking off to find the runner placements. Bold climbing has always been an integral part of Northumberland climbing and On the Verge certainly fitted into this category. I cleaned it off and was able to convince myself that if I got too gripped on the upper part of the arete I would be able to jump down onto the ledge on my right. Fortunately I did not have to put it to the test.

Kyloe Out was the sleeping giant and soft option to Kyloe In, with many superb and contrasting routes, from Nev Hannaby's superb wall climb Tacitation to Two Tier Buttress with the Alan Austin classic Coldstream Corner. The trees adjacent to the crag were smaller and much less intrusive in those days and the turf beneath the crag made bouldering (landing) and picnicking much more pleasant than perhaps they are today.

The nature of the crag was changed forever, however, when Bob Hucthinson made the first ascent of Australia Crack, which was probably the sandbag of all time at 6a (that is apart from all of the Smith's routes at Callerhues). Bob's ascent was done around the time of the 'Great Chalk Debate' and was chalk free which definitely reduced the options on the crux. The day I did an early repeat I jumped five or six times from the crux before summoning the courage to make the precarious crux move on greasy jams and layaways. This could account for my recent arthroscopy.

In the mid 1970s Bob Hutchinson and I (who around that time had the new route scene more or less to ourselves) started to hear rumours of two brothers who were very fit and very bold and according to Hedley Smith (no relation) were going to give us some competition in the future – he was not wrong. I first met Bob and Tommy Smith at the Cradlewell and discovered them to be extremely intense regarding their climbing, immediately recognising kindred spirits in respect of competitiveness and new routing. I seem to remember spending one of those first nights arguing grades with Bob – some things haven't changed. The Smith brothers opened their new route account with the development of Callerhues, a superb bouldering crag where even the VS's are 5b and they started to run riot in North Northumberland with ascents such as Lost Cause, Barbarian, Judge, Jury and Rajah.

Another local, Steve Blake, who was then probably in his late teens, started to make an impression and in 1978 he teamed up with Bob and a bag of chalk to climb Original Sin, a bold route in the quarry at Kyloe Out. Steve was very fit, with strong fingers and was into bouldering and boulder problems rather than routes, even in those early days. He added a companion route to Australia Crack – Prime Time and he did a number of new routes on the Bowden and Kyloe crags. The legacy he left all future boulderers however was Hitch Hikers, an incredibly hard fingery problem which was some years ahead of its time. The shallow pockets for the feet necessitated Steve wearing an EB on one foot and a Robbins boot on the other foot, or so he said.

Bob Hutchinson's last new route in the County, a few days before his death, on Eagle Crag in the Lake District in 1978, was Hard Reign, which aptly described a golden era which ended so abruptly and tragically.

After Bob's untimely death and Tommy Smith's first and second early retirements, Bob Smith, Paul Stewart, Ian Kyle and I regularly climbed together. Bob Hutchinson and I had first met Paul a few years earlier. He was highly talented and extremely flexible and could, for example, literally put his foot above his head and then proceed to rock over. He was subsequently nicknamed 'bendy legs' by that old stiffy Bob Smith. Around this time he did the first ascent of Bad Company, the day after he had been pipped to the first ascent of Bad Finger by Bob Hutchinson. Although he did hard climbing in the Lake District his real love was outcrop climbing and his contribution included the intimidating Outward Bound, Troubleshooter – a technical wall climb and Autowind – an interesting slab climb. In the days before sticky boots, precise footwork and flexibility were essential on Troubleshooter, although a pile of pine needles was helpful to break the fall on abortive attempts.

Ian Kyle was an ex-rugby player with strong fingers and good footwork who slimmed down to become an extremely competitive and technical climber and who climbed 'Y' Climb, left hand finish, but whose piece de resistance was the rarely repeated Belford Pie Shop.

Peter Kirton was another young Northumbrian who developed a national reputation for his extreme power, which he directed more towards boulder problems in the County than routes, although he did climb the Direct Finish to Fosbury Flop at Selby's Cove with Andy Moss. Vienna, a desperate boulder problem start to Bob Smith's Rising Damp was more his forte.

It was about this time that I snatched the County's first elbow injury and had to give the powerful bouldering a miss. Bob and Peter, however, would be hard at it all day scraping their chalk bags in the dust in an attempt to burn arse. Now Peter had the edge on the power but Bob had more stamina, was a lot more flexible and probably more competitive. It was always difficult to know who had won, the rules and the interpretation of them being so complicated.

From 1978 up until beyond the publication of the 1989 guide Bob Smith dominated Northumberland climbing with an impressive string of first ascents, many at the very highest standard, often with poor protection and done with minimal cleaning and pre-inspection. In 1981, however, he really did take

Northumberland climbing a major step forward when he attacked the 'impossible' overhanging walls at the left end of Back Bowden. By this time Bob and I climbed almost exclusively as a team and consequently I held his rope and seconded most of his climbs in this area. The most memorable, from my point of view, being on Macbeth. This comes out from the cave towards the right side of the wall on big underclings to make a difficult landing on the lip beneath the overhanging wall, makes a short traverse right and then climbs the middle of the wall by means of some very sequency moves. I got over the lip, with Bob belaying me from the ground to enable him to give me the numbers on the tricky bit, using an extra rope to reach from the belay on a small sapling some 100 feet back through the heather to the edge of the crag with a second rope used as my top rope. Well, in spite of the excellent advice I managed to cock-up the moves and fell off from the crux probably 20 – 25 feet up. I fell gracefully through the air (believe that if you will) to land daintily on the ground on the stretch of the rope. I managed it at the second attempt. In 1983 Bob showed his immense versatility and to some extent unorthodox approach by springing to reach the pot hole and flake half way up the wall just left of His Eminence to produce Poverty, a route that has had only one known repeat to this day, unlike Kremlin and Second Born which remain unrepeated.

Most of the new routing that Bob and I did in the County was done on Wednesday evenings after work or during the winter months. One such evening ascent was Rough Passage in 1988 which climbs the wall left of Poseidon and then surmounts the wave by some very bold and poorly protected climbing. Falling off from 25 feet when in a horizontal position with minimal gear is not recommended. The main season was spent climbing in all areas of the UK and from 1980 onwards throughout Europe. Much of our time was spent climbing in the Lake District and in the mid-80s we were invited to join the FRCC only to discover that this was so that we could re-write the Eastern Crags guide and so from 1985 – 87 we spent even more time in the Lakes, or to be precise, the Eastern Fells. We did in fact stall somewhat the commencement of work on the 1989 Northumberland guide to enable us to complete the Eastern Crags guide.

Many excellent new routes had been done in the late eighties, including some by climbers little mentioned so far in this article. In February, 1987 Tommy Smith, during one of his comebacks, he has had as many as Status Quo, climbed Elder Brother at Kyloe Out, a hard and serious companion route to 'The Younger Brothers' First Born. On this route Tom was accompanied by Tim Gallagher, a powerful young climber from South Shields. In 1986 at Kyloe In, Tim, this time accompanied by Tom, climbed up the futuristic wall to the right of High T to give High Society. Karl and Graham Telfer are two local climbers who have been very active in Northumberland for many years. There was a period when Karl and Graham frequently claimed the first ascent of a route that Bob Hutchinson and I had climbed a week or two earlier. This did give them, however, a number of hard second ascents, including Endless Flight. They have now added many hard routes of their own, including Charlotte's Dream and Ruth's Route.

Just prior to the 1989 guide two hard new routes were climbed using modern techniques by: Tony Coutts with Peak Techniques and by Mark Liptrot with the Railway Children. Bob joined in with his superb On the Rocks, the technical and serious wall below the Tube traverse – flexibility, strong fingers and big balls are essential requirements.

Once the Northumberland guide was put to bed it was quite a relief to be guidebook free and Bob and I concentrated on other areas, leaving the new routes gauntlet to be picked up by Hugh Harris, Karl and Graham Telfer, Stephen Roberts, Malcolm Smith and others. The details are to be found in a later chapter of this book. Meanwhile, let us hope that the ethics adopted by climbers doing new routes in the future go some way to matching those of the earlier generations. We have in Northumberland a tradition for good hard and serious climbing without resorting to chipping, pegging or glueing etc. Please help it continue.

Northumberland's Lost Crag – A Personal Perspective
Andy Birtwistle

Once upon a time there was The Belling – it is no more. Rather, from a climber's perspective it is no more, for a few feet of rock are still visible sandwiched between the dark green of the forest and the still darker waters of Kielder Reservoir. It is the lost crag of the County and no amount of access negotiations can bring it back. Its fate was sealed forever, its death entwined with that of all the upper reaches of the North Tyne Valley. A sacrifice, meant to bring life to the ailing industries of Tyneside and Teeside, but in hindsight only an expensive recreation facility. Kielder Water is a testament to the over ambitious plans of the 70's. And the crag is gone.

Many folk have never heard of the Belling. To the older ones amongst us it probably brings back memories of pleasant days out but it was never a major crag by any means. Not so the majesty of Simonside and Ravensheugh or the magic of Kyloe. It was an ordinary little crag, but to me it is very special because it was here that I was introduced to a sport that would change my life.

My initiation was unforeseen. During a weekend away, with canoeing on the agenda, the river level was low and, after an abortive day looking for something resembling a rapid, my arm was twisted to join a group of climbers for the Sunday. Grumbling and mumbling something about not being able to see the point of finding a hard way up when I could walk around, I complied. I have never looked back.

The crag itself was of compact sandstone with a gritty texture, about 60 feet high. The routes, about two dozen, were mostly climbed by I Richardson in the early 60s and apparently quite a lot of gardening was required. Later the Kielder Field Study Centre developed the crag as a practice ground and regular traffic kept the lines clean. These lines were mostly on the slabby side of vertical with some excellent cracks.

The aspect was wonderful. On the edge of the forest overlooking the pastures of the North Tyne and facing due south, it was the perfect beginners' crag and climbable all year round. Not absorbed by the dense trees, it stood proud in a setting of bracken, heather and isolated Scots Pine with a sheep grazed grassy base. Easy access along the disused North Tyne railway meant you could drive almost to its foot but its remoteness guaranteed a secluded and peaceful setting. An isolated pinnacle provided a practice area and the routes themselves ranged from Difficult to HVS.

My very first rock climb was a Hard V Diff called Set. Vibrams on the feet (magic boots were strictly for the experts), cable laid rope tied round the waist with a bowline and, of course, no chalk. I loved it. The expert Ed Williams led the route and one by one we were led like lambs to the slaughter. Taking it in turn we laughed and cajoled each other to better the previous unfortunate's performance. The undercut start awkwardly gained a ledge which was followed by an exquisite semi-layback finishing up an airy wall. It was brilliant and I was hooked.

Later visits revealed other delights. The classic was a fine crack up the centre of the Great Slab. It was a Very Severe called Thin and in those days VS meant it. I have a wonderful photo of myself awkwardly seconding the route, a bumblie before the days of bumblies.

Another great route was Ra. At Mild VS it provided delicate slab climbing. Merle Crack and The Shriek were only Hard Severe and some of my first leads. Real testers at a time when I was learning the ropes.

The hardest route on the crag was a well named gem! Diamond was hard. Given 5b in the 1979 guide it was both bold and delicate with a strenuous mantleshelf to get you started. I dreamed of leading routes like this.

We paid a few visits in the late 70's aware of the fact that soon it would be no more, even doing the girdle traverse 120 feet of climbing with hanging belays! Just prior to its death by drowning the cream team mopped up any remaining lines for completeness but it will always be remembered for its great middle grade routes and its lovely location.

For me personally it evokes much more because unknowingly it provided me with 20 years of fun and adventure and it introduced me to a way of life and friends that will last a lifetime.

Stones on Simonside
Martin Cooper

Millions of years ago this was a beach,
Waves lapping on coastal shore,
Sand pressed down beneath.
Pressure of sea, air and time.
Years too many for mere human mind to fathom
Pressing down on sand.

Now we stand on rocks with sea 15 miles eastwards.
Could this once have been sea shore,
With fish swimming serenely by?
What force of time or nature
Raised this beach, turned sand to rock,
Salty grains to smooth rugged faces
Where now we climb?

We too will be forced down from here
By night fall, hunger and cold.
While rocks remain above,
Standing up in straight strong rows
Guarding silently the hill all night,
Where once was beach.

County Ethics
Dave Cuthbertson

When I was asked to write an article on Northumberland climbing as seen through the eyes of a raider from the frozen North, my immediate thought was one of slight confusion. How on earth can I possibly be considered a raider on my own land! I thought to myself. You see the problem is that the Scots have always viewed Northumberland as a No-Mans Land rather than an English county. There is nothing new in this belief for attempts have been made to keep out the marauding Scot since the building of Hadrian's Wall. However, the English must have seriously underestimated the Scots' yearning for what must be the finest sandstone in the British Isles. Otherwise they would have built the wall 70 miles further north! These days, of course, a more effective deterrent comes in the guise of Northumberland Hard Man Bob Smith, whose new route development and ethical influence in the County is almost unparalleled. Note the word 'hard' because it is not only in the area of putting up difficult first ascents for which Bob is famed but also his association with back street brawls in the city of Newcastle. The stories of Bob and his brother Tommy are now legendary and woe betide anyone who dares cross lines with the Smiths! (This explains why 99% of all new routes have been accredited to Bob – only joking!)

Over the last 20 years climbing in general has made some tremendous advances, but not only in the field of high standard rockclimbing. We have seen an increasing number of indoor climbing walls, the European competition circuit hit the British scene, regional leagues have sprung up all over the country and last but not least the ever controversial subject of bolted sport climbs. As a natural consequence there has been a dramatic increase in the number of people climbing. "The fastest growing sport next to walking", I read recently. The question of whether or not these trends are to your liking is really another subject entirely. What is so refreshing to me personally is that the County quietly continues its involvement at the cutting edge of rockclimbing. It is the epitome of all the ingredients for which British climbing is so renowned, naturally protected, bold, athletic, technical and in its own modest way, adventurous.

Climbing in Northumberland has survived all these influences – it has come through almost completely unscathed. Only Bowden Doors on a sunny Sunday afternoon compares with its Welsh and Peak District counterparts in terms of popularity, and that is only because it is one of the few crags where you don't have to boulder above 6a to get off the ground on VDiffs and Severes!

Scotland's participation in the development of Northumberland climbing does not really compare to the contributions made by local climbers. Its involvement is more of a tradition of weekend and mid week jaunts by various enthusiastic Edinburgh groups. However the first ascents which have been put up, particularly the most recent, are not only of the highest calibre in terms of quality but also significant pointers to the future.

The first time I heard about the quality of the climbing was in the early 70s after Murray Hamilton had been to Kyloe and Bowden crags. Tales of the incredible jam cracks, undercut roofs and overhanging walls of impeccable pocketed rock. "You'll love it" said Murray, "It's just made for Cubule Machines" (a term I was known as by Murray at that time). I couldn't wait. My first trip, in fact, was with the veteran south west climber Ian Duckworth. Ian was a big bearded, burley mischievous character, an ex-mariner, the man responsible for the lives of the crew on Tilman's Mischief. He was a self confessed sandstone addict and like many grit and sandstone climbers, he had developed an uncanny boldness which I suspect was based on a philosophy which can be related to the diminutive stature of the crags, that if all else fails there was always the possibility of surviving a ground fall! Ian pointed me at

Monty Pythons at Kyloe In The Wood. It was quite magical. The fairy tale theme of route naming and the eerie enchanted ambience of the surrounding forest has left a lasting impression to this very day. I did Monty Pythons on that first visit (direct, not via the crack to the right). What a fantastic problem, pulling into an Egyptian (back and foot) using the chickenhead and a one finger pocket, then slapping for the sloping pinch – a bit of a shuffle, heel up, rock over for the pocket with your left hand and finish with a couple of stonking jams – a classic 6b problem.

I suppose Murray and I were the first of a new generation in Scotland and unfortunately, having already introduced chalk to Scotland, we were now held responsible for bringing it to the County. Murray climbed Roof Route Direct at Back Bowden and I added The Rack which was claimed at a later date and called Poison Dwarf. We climbed many other routes thinking they were first ascents. Routes such as Red Rum, Bad Company, Harp Direct, the various roofs to the left of the Sorcerer, Transformer, Brutally Handsome, Sunshine Superman and many more. That's all history now. What is more important are the friendships which develop over cold winter weekends. Memories of evenings at Kyloe in the Wood hiding in damp ditches to escape the search lights of disgruntled landowners.

Although many other climbers from Scotland became devotees of Northumberland climbing, the ones familiar to me were the likes of Murray, Kenny Spence, Spider McKenzie and from the south was the determined and forceful late Bob Hutchinson. Cool hand John Earl and that dynamic ball of energy Bob Smith. There were others less familiar to me at that time. Bill Wayman, Graham and Karl Telfer, and Steve Blake. As seemed normal in Northumberland, we rarely put the rope on, preferring to solo many of the routes or go bouldering.

In the late 70s I moved away from Edinburgh and consequently lost touch with the Northumberland scene. By the mid-80s climbing had taken a few radical steps and the significance of bouldering in high standard climbing at last gained the respect it deserved. Inspirational in all this were possibly the likes of America's John Gill, John Bacher and Ron Kauk. In Britain Jerry Moffat often bouldered with local Pete Kirton to help improve his power. Pete left a legacy of hard problems and unfinished projects. His most famous (completed) problem being Vienna at Bowden Doors, but many other more powerful and more interesting problems could be found lurking in the darkest corners beneath the various roofs which abound the Northumberland crags.

While working in the South I naturally found myself drawn once again to the solitude and quiet of the Northumberland moors, I repeated Bob Smith's Macbeth taking a nice flyer from the top break when a hold snapped. Fortunately a friend held. Murray climbed the traverse at Kyloe in the Woods from Crack of Gloom to Elf – a particularly fine effort. At Back Bowden I traversed the crimpy wall, starting at the left end of the Macbeth wall and continuing under the lowest roofs beneath The Arches. Under the Sorcerer I climbed the low level pocket traverse going left to right to give an excellent 6c problem, but harder for the short. From a sitting start the roof leading directly up to the final groove of Black Magic is another worthy addition to this section of crag, providing some powerful climbing. At Kyloe in the Woods I climbed an overhanging crack now known as the Yorkshireman and of course that classic of the crag, Hitchhikers.

In 1989 I added County Ethics E7, 7a to the left end of the Macbeth wall. This was the first time I top roped a new route before leading it but it is an excellent climb and worthy of its grade. The route is so called because I was going to pre-place the only runner but after speaking to Bob, who dutifully said, "You've got to place it on the lead, County ethics lad" – that's what I did, survived the jump on my first attempt, succeeded on my second go and felt very satisfied at having paid my dues.

By the early 90s a number of talented young up and coming climbers came and went and with them went the camaraderie and inspiration which I found so important to survive in Scottish climbing. Mark McGowan, Graeme Livingstone and the late Colin Gilchrist to name but a few and now the phenomenon, Malcolm Smith. "The boy is strong, I mean we are talking strong here Cubby". The sincere words of steel fingers Kenny Spence. Intrigued and not yet as fit as I should be after a season's guiding I swallowed my pride and went to visit Malcolm at his parent's house in Dunbar. Climbing on wood was a new experience. It was excellent and I was very impressed at the problems. Another young climber was also there, Stuart Cameron. We had a great session and once again I felt inspired and as competitive as ever. Although Malcolm's strength is now second to none, at the time I could usually hold my own and in some cases even burn him off. The big news was that Malc had done Hitchhikers Direct. We organised a day out together and I almost flashed it. I got it on my second or third attempt. It is a superb problem which you have to do with a sitting start. Malc then showed me all these other sitting starts he had added to the established classics at Kyloe in the Wood. The project for the day was a low level traverse coming in from the Pearler and finishing up the Yorkshireman. I fell off at the last move (but managed it on another trip), but more importantly I realised that my training on the Fort William wall and our new wooden wall in Kinlochleven had more than translated to real rock. Malc went on to climb the pocket traverse, There and Back at Back Bowden – a fine achievement and also on-sight soloed The Rajah, Merlin and The Tube Extension and repeated a few nasty existing climbs such as When The Wind Blows, Charlotte's Dream and On The Rocks. At Back Bowden he completed Smiths Lip, an eliminate traverse along the lip of the lowest roof beneath the Arches. I climbed the arete direct from beneath the roof (also beneath the Arches) to give a classic problem and at Kyloe in the Woods I completed an earlier Kirton project by traversing the low lying roof between Crack of Gloom and the Pearler to give Cubby's Lip. This gives an excellent piece of climbing.

The two by far most impressive feats of climbing that I have seen recently are Malcolm's complete traverse of Kyloe in the Wood, Leviathan, with the crux on a newly extended section between Hitchhikers and the Rack, the last move on a boulder problem which is over 50 metres long. This is a truly world class problem and will no doubt achieve international acclaim. The other is the prow above The Duke of York, Transcendence, and weighs in at an incredible E9 7a. Top roped, of course, before it was led, this is the most significant pointer to the future since Bob Smith did On The Rocks.

Finally it has to be said that all these desperate climbs and boulder problems are paled into insignificance by comparison to the nerve wracking, out of body after dinner speech experience at the Northumbrian Mountaineering Club dinner. Imagine two rows of tables containing 150 members in dinner suits and evening dress and two scruffy smelly climbers, one the guest speaker and the other his mate, having just hitched 200 miles in the pouring rain after a week's dossing and climbing in Stoney Middleton and nothing between them but 50p.

A tip to any young up-start. If you can cope with an after dinner speech then the world is your oyster, but just remember don't be taken in by the "Oh there will only be about 20 to 30 climbers dressed in jeans and Helly Hansen" ploy. I was!

Geordies – "Keepers of the County"
Bob Smith

In the beginning (early 70's BC – before cheating) there were two distinct breeds of climbers. There were adventurers, nice chappies who looked for classic challenges, be they in the Alps or Northumberland. They enjoyed their days out on the crags and enjoyed themselves in the evenings, chatting quietly over a tot or two. On the other hand there was us. Our breed went out training and trained for specific routes or moves and got tanked up in the evening to boot, having wild arguments about grades, stars, style, class etc. These often broke out into skirmishes with pushing, pulling and a lot of verbal abuse, such as "You talk a load of crap, son" or "Nash off, you divvy, before I pull your head off. Anyway stuff this arguing and get the beers in, it's your turn you tight fisted git". Anyway enough about Tommy and me. Okay, so how did it all start? I will tell you a little about the old days.

I was introduced, or seduced, into climbing by my brother Tommy. He was fresh from living in London and knew all about sandstone climbing as he had climbed at Harrison's Rocks, Stone Farm and Bowles Rocks, all in the South East. He was nearly a cockney but I was soon to correct that.

Anyway, things went through the normal channels, Crag Lough, The Wanneys, Simonside, lovely isn't it? Then like a bolt of lightening out of the blue Hutchinson and Earl came to our attention in the form of a blue new route book, "The Blue Bible". Well, was this to change things or WHAT? No wonder we started drinking? This nightmare in blue had all sorts of horrible and embarrassing things in it. Things like 5a, 5b, 5c, "5c, they must be Gods! and we are just two Smiths". But as anyone knows two Smiths are a match for any bugger. So we set off on our quest, not asking too much at first, only to be the best climbing brothers in the world (just kidding, ha ha). Anyway we got our teeth into this book and by God did this book bite back. It had more bite than a Jock eating haggis or a haggis eating Jock. Getting back to our exploits, as we worked our way through the book, some good routes, some not so good. Then we stepped up our efforts. By this time we had twigged on that some sort of training was a must. We went from 4c to 5a and, believe me, in those days that was a Neil Armstrong type step. As time passed the training got more serious, Jesmond Dene morning, afternoon and night, bullworkers, hanging from door lintels, boozing, Tommy's outside wall in sunny, downtown Byker.

Around this time a new concept was to hit us, Concordia. Not just a climbing wall, it was to become an arena, a place to show your talents and give everyone else a hard time (some things never change). This new wall brought all sorts of people to the surface, people like Martin Moran and Steve Blake. Now this lad Blake knew about training. He would traverse the full length of the wall using only the mortar joints for fingers and feet. His party piece was climbing upside down with his head fifteen feet above the concrete deck. A few suckers fell prey to this trick and found themselves with large bumps on their heads. Concordia was also a place to see what Bob and John were up to but, as expected they were still kicking arse. So we went on the drink. What else was there to do?

After a few weeks or months of this training regime one thing was starting to emerge. We could climb well and had plenty of neck and when I say neck, we're talking giraffe here – jumping 30 feet off Bowden Doors time after time and living to tell the tale. As we worked our way through the good Bible, climbing became an unstoppable obsession for me. At this time we heard a whisper of a new guide soon to be published. Well you can imagine the adrenaline rush. All hell was let loose. Never before or since in the North East have so many wire and nylon brushes been purchased by so few (have a cigar, Bob). Tommy and I raided up and down the County, from freeing The Dangler at Causey Quarry at six in the morning to new routes at Crag Lough in the evening. Our big breakthrough was Callerhues. This was to be a major turning point in our climbing, hard work, hard routes, hard drinking. We were ecstatic. We got some extreme routes which were just the spur we needed. I remember Tommy once saying, "It's not runners they will need on this crag, but bog paper". On the publication of the 1979 guide we had done well. Callerhues had got a good selection of routes in. We also had a big fistful of hard routes in the main guide and more in the recent additions section.

During this very hectic period we had to cope with the raiders. From the North came Dave Cuthbertson (Cubbie), Murray Hamilton, Kenny Spence and Spider McKenzie. Now these lads had climbed in the County for years, untethered and undetected, disguised as sheep rustlers and scarecrows with out sized wellies (or was it just skinny legs) – now they blew their whistle on Monty Python's Flying Circus. They were caught red-handed with their kilts up. Tell tale chalk marks – the first in the County – and traces of wool started a mini war. But in time the Jocks became friends with the Geordies, but underneath the Jocks were unhappy living in fear and only raiding for new routes under the cover of darkness.

This was enough to contend with but we also had bandits coming from the west in the form of Pete Whillance, Dave Armstrong, Pete Botterill and Jeff Lamb, to mention but a few. The latter of these, the late Jeff Lamb, was a right wolf in sheep's clothing. A few of the classic routes poached from under our very noses were The Manta at Bowden, Over the Edge at Simonside and Impossible Wall at Crag Lough. Thank God the others concentrated on the Lakes or who knows what other gems would have fallen to the expert raiders from the west.

We also had to cope with Yorkshire Terriers. These were vicious animals with big backs in their own territory but quite harmless in the County, content with chasing after second and third ascents and leaving with big smiles, but taking nothing of value. One way of keeping raiders out of the County was to hit their areas, doing their routes. So Yorkshire and the Lakes became regular weekend venues. While Jeff Lamb was raiding Northumberland he cleaned off The Barbarian which was hastily climbed by myself and witnessed by a bunch of Picts, Sporrans and all. I don't recall Jeff Lamb raiding for any more routes after that. I think everyone went home and guarded their own territory!

At the back end of the 70s and during the early 80s we had built up a formidable squad of "Geordie Guardians", comprising of myself, Tommy Smith, John Earl, Paul Stewart, Steve Blake and later on, Andy Birtwistle, Ian Kyle, Andy Moss, Colin Murley and, guarding everything below 15 feet, Peter "The Boulderer" Kirton. Other teams operating at this time had also matured into a forceful and potent group, led by Karl and Graham Telfer and helped out by Paul Saville and Martin Doyle. Around this time it was realised that a supplement to the 79 guide would be needed as a hundred or more routes had been climbed. This again sparked a new rush of activity, only this time the bulk of the routes would be done by Geordies – the Keepers of the County. The supplement and what followed was to be the making of the County. Northumberland had now established itself as a major climbing area in the country, offering routes both bold and protected on whinstone and sandstone. The particular attraction of the sandstone being routes of a gymnastic nature as well as bouldering second to none in the country. After the publication of the 1989 guide our group began to move further afield, leaving the County in the very capable hands of Hugh Harris, John Wallace, Steve Roberts and others. They in turn have left a legacy of excellent classics, too many to mention.

So that's the Smith version of the history of climbing in Northumberland, but what of the future? First, let's take a quick look at the reasons for the massive improvements in the past few years. Training is undoubtedly the most important. This in itself has undergone some dramatic changes, from short bouldering workouts on viaducts with Tilley lamps or night visits to Corby's equipped with pram, car battery and car head lights, as some did, or soloing at places like Causey Quarry in the evenings – to the long days bouldering in the north of the County, where traversing at a high standard was achieved, 6c and above. New found areas near to towns have offered excellent and very rewarding training, for example, Frenchman's Cove near South Shields, with its ever changing character, offering endless problems, from ferocious roofs, overhanging stamina trips, to finger testing crimping. There is also the sheltered Lumley Bridge, with its 60 metre long finger traversing wall, at different levels. Climbers now also have some first class all weather climbing walls Eldon, Concordia and Whickham Thorns, to mention just a few. Some enthusiasts also have DIY custom built walls made to their own specifications, designer walls inside their own homes.

The change in climbers' ethics and tactics in the last few years is probably one of the biggest contributory factors towards the rise in the standard of new bold routes. Top-roping, which only a few years ago would have been treated with extreme contempt, is now accepted as normal. The preplacing of runners is another modern approach which leaves a lot to the imagination and to the integrity and honesty of the individual. For example, how long is a sling? Is the preplaced protection actually on the route being climbed? These are the types of question which need answering honestly.

In the past the majority of routes were climbed using various tactics, the best obviously being on sight without being cleaned and, believe me, the bulk of routes were done in this fashion but as grades became harder routes were cleaned by abseil and checked over to see if they had holds or not and, it goes without saying, some routes were top roped prior to the first ascent. However, this was not a common practice. I remember climbers trying the tops of some of the harder problems in winter when there were large snow drifts at the bottom of the route so a soft landing was guaranteed, or just jumping off and taking their chance. Well I don't think the modern breed, having more sense, has to go through that or would even want to.

So what's for the future? Well, hopefully, if things continue in the same mode as described above climbing in Northumberland should look something like this: long sustained and bold routes at Sandy Crag, Ravensheugh, Back and Front Bowden or even on the sea cliffs at Fast Castle and at Spittle Quarry; long sustained boulder problems linking up existing traverses with the blank areas being breached, with no resting, and the odd 7a or 7b upwards (British grades) thrown in, just to keep you interested; also sitting starts to problems which, in some cases, can make an individual problem so much harder. These are some of the more obvious and more satisfying steps into the future. Let us hope the ugly face of climbing – chipping, bolting, pegging or using resin on our outcrops and crags never rears its head again. Or is there a case for bolting up unused quarries or unprotectable or loose seacliffs?

Which brings us to a new dimension, never before encountered in Northumberland, the use of Sika. This compound can be used for the prevention or creation of a problem or route. Originally its use was to reinstate a broken off hold to its former state – glueing the hold back on. Unfortunately this can be interpreted in different ways. Here are a few examples; filling in cracks or holes, preventing would be ascensionists using or doing moves differently to the first ascensionist, preventing a hold which had not yet broken off from breaking off or, the more blatant approach, using Sika to create or enhance a hold. Right or wrong will depend on your personal viewpoint, but you must ask yourself this question – why did we build climbing walls? Or is it simply "needs must where the Devil drives?" So the moral of the story is, leave it the way you found it. After all, someone, one day might ask you, "What of the future of Northumberland"!

Well as darkness approaches I feel tired and my rheumatism is working itself again, so I think I will put my feet up, smoke my pipe and read the newspaper while stroking the dog, watching the hot embers on the fire fade from the corner of my watering eye. Yawn. As I fade into slumber my mind drifts and I recall golden days gone by. Then, with a start I remember I had better get down to the pub for some booze and chat with the lads before I get too old. See you on the crags lads and lasses!

First Among Equals – An Obsession
Hugh Harris

A fatal error in my schooling – a geography teacher that added flesh to the bones of an idea. My youthful attraction to all things vertical or, dangerous was crystallised by Karl Telfer. That first opportunity to experience the "real thing" was an embryonic first trip to Causey Quarry late in June 1982 that tipped an already lazy schoolboy, bored to tears with 'A' levels, over the edge into a world of obsession, a life dominated by the pursuit of rock climbing. A local quarry up the road from my parents had aided the level of interest. I can clearly remember from the age of eight soloing around, up and down walls, admittedly easy, up to 60 or 70 feet in height. A crazy thing for a young kid to do but entirely natural to me! Hard Rock – the original black and white version – specially borrowed from the local library at the age of 12 or 13 was the published inspiration. Not for me the football heroes of the time or the pop stars but an unknown man called Joe Brown on the greatest aspiration route of all – the natural line crying out to be climbed – Cenotaph Corner. It's so funny looking back. I still haven't managed The Corner but I guess aspirations change …

Almost seven years ago to the day and I find myself on a Tuesday evening dash some eighty miles from work in Redcar, via Jeff's, to pick him up in his capacity as faithful belayer.

Obsessions are, I find, better when shared.

The previous weekend's attempt on the line had failed three or four times halfway through the infuriating crux – an injured finger from my second day's climbing at Buoux on a recent French trip contributing greatly. After spending two hours cleaning the route and working out the moves in cloudy, fog shrouded conditions, neither Dave, who had accompanied as belayer on that occasion and was bored senseless and very cold, or myself really had the drive to make it happen. The wrench, the shear heart ache to have to walk away, knowing you can do it but above all, knowing other people can do it as well. How was I going to wait till next weekend …?

The walk-up, usually a forty five minute shamble turns into a thirty minute jog. The chalk, carefully cleaned off at close of play on Saturday to leave no clues, had not returned. A vague unease, a growing feeling of paranoia, a so subtle pressure was consuming me.

It had to happen today.

A quick abseil, rope round a bollard belay, to brush the crucial holds then flick it out of reach. A boulder around to warm up.

Then just sit, mentally prepare with time to reflect …

I first visited Ravensheugh on a sweltering day in July 1984 with John Wallace and another friend who lived down the road. We had seen the cover of the '79 guide and had heard of the reputation of the crag and finally psyched up to the walk-in. That wasn't too bad but the crag was incredibly intimidating. A struggle up Pendulum convinced us that routes were not going to succumb easily. After having a mooch around and managing to somehow reach the top of the second pinnacle we looked back toward Ravensheugh Crack and were stunned by the obvious and, to us, totally unclimbable line to its left with an elusive chicken head on the top wall. God that would be hard! A bit of research in the Wilderness Ways new routes book later that week informed us that it was yet another three star 'Linfoot' route. So that was impossible then! We had obviously been bitten by the bug and returned the following weekend to do battle with Easter Grooves, Baluster Crack and The Trouser Legs. The line was temporarily forgotten …

Five years later, and a copy of the new, hot off the press, Northumberland Guide rested in my sweaty paw. Bang! Right between the eyes. The photo of Andy Birtwistle on Ravensheugh Crack with an obvious, very real, line of apparently useable holds to his left – the spark to set the flame.

The intervening five years had seen my climbing go through mixed fortunes. A different addiction to the delights of the female of the species had interrupted climbing far too much but that addiction, much to Alison's disgust was dying a speedy death – the poor girl never did understand and could never accept.

The addiction to newness was growing and all consuming. There is no logic to the situation – how important can 35 feet of unclimbed rock become? The personal challenge is blown out of all proportion. The guide had clarified where the real gaps were – the standard "Bob's probably done it" no longer sufficed.

A visit to Ravensheugh was becoming the most important fact in my whole life. Work colleagues scratched quizzical heads and muttered "crazy man". The first solo foray armed with cleaning gear was interrupted by the presence of Gavin, John and Pudsie, ensconced at the crag with a rope down The Judas Hole. After watching proceedings for a while and borrowing a crucial bomb proof No 4 Tri-cam I managed a flash of the route. You can hardly call it an on sight when you've watched someone top rope the route in front of you! An on sight of Plumbline was thwarted by lichen covered holds at the top, so, after a quick clean and check out of the holds the ascent became a formality. The boys put a rope down the wall right of Billy Biscuit and gave it a brush off. Totally devoid of protection and with a high crux it eventually got a top rope ascent from Gavin after various chicken heads snapped off, pushing the technical grade up. I was offered the rope for a "quick try". I flashed it! The gauntlet was lain down – could it be soloed? Gavin declined the offer and I took it up with a Lapse of Reason – a suitable name for the circumstances and a very good route.

Still the other line waited …

Enough of this reverie, there's a route to be climbed.

I know the rack for the route by heart. The crucial runner is a DMM wallnut zero – the same one that took the falls four days ago – just above half height. The gear below that is very good but a fall from higher up would leave you close to the ground, closer still if that crucial runner ripped. The start up Ravensheugh crack is typical HVS ground – a bit graunchy – and leads you to the overhung ledge below the start of the independent line. The first runners go in and protect the awkward pull around into the crack. A few more crack moves lead to a six inch square ledge – a good hand hold or a good foothold but getting from one position to the other again proves awkward. I marvel at how small that zero really is, especially in relatively soft rock, as I carefully place it! It is possible to stand here in relative comfort but time just rots the brain and I'm running out of chalk through nervous reflexive dipping.

Go for broke – this time the weather's good, I'm feeling good and by God the route's the best!

Step up to the right onto a rounded edge then back left, right foot smearing desperately in the shallow corner, right hand, finger complaining, crimping the tiny edge, a long, long move to the tiny pocket – my God I held it – that didn't happen on the last attempts – quickly followed by another pocket and another long reach to a good break – got the depression first time.

Pause for thought, time to consider that long ago forgotten chicken head – the red herring. You don't use it. It says please try me but I know its little game.

A high foot into the break and a third long reach gains the top holds – a mere formality.

Oh joyous release. The pressure comes off – Jeff says "It's too hard for him" and "Why don't I ab for the gear". The cleaning rope is belayed close at hand so I clip in and ab back down, removing gear as I go, Jeff runs round to drop the rope. I touch ground, the merest flick looses the rope and my ashen faced belayer informs me that perhaps the wind had loosened the rope from around the flat bollard.

"First Among Equals" could have had a very different ending or maybe never been written! Climbing's dangerous, but so is obsession. One is very good at masking the other.

My first E6 had been memorable – a perfect line, one of the best in the County so eloquently putting John Earl's introduction and the guide in which it is written out of date. It's a brave man who says "Most of the good lines on the major crags have now been climbed …"

The illness still remains, just in repose waiting for the next relapse, waiting …

Now what about the photos opposite pages 192, 264 and the front and back covers …?

Crag Lough
Hilary Porteus

A curlew calls, a lofty cackling,
Above the walls of whinstone, beckoning,
The misty morn unveiling, laying bare,
The crag beneath Hadrians wall.

The Climbers came, exploring, challenging,
Their new routes claimed, their laughter echoing,
Now polished rock faced north, remembering,
The sieges and plunders of old.

The Lough laps grey, the dry grass rustling,
Another day, the walkers bustling,
A Pewit whines, a climber stands aloft,
A crown on a ribbon of stone.

As evenings fall the darkness gathering,
The rucksacks packed, the ropes unravelling,
The crag stands proud, above the moorland bare,
And faces its future alone.

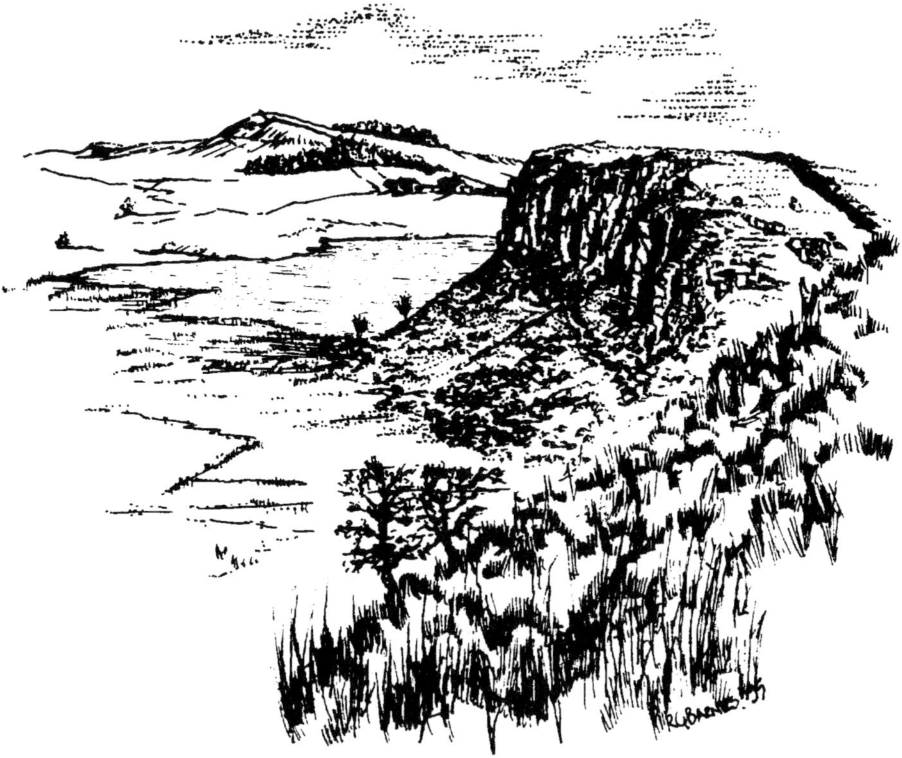

From Northumberland to K2 ... and back
Alan Hinkes

"As I heard the avalanche thundering down, I realised this one had my name on it. I dived out of my tent and grabbed the fixed rope attached to the vertical wall opposite – as wet heavy snow crushed the tent. I could hardly breathe and was being sucked away by the tremendous force of falling snow and huge blocks of ice. I only just escaped with my life."

This incident occurred on the north side of K2, far remote from a place which had played a major part in the development of my mountaineering career, my native north country.

At the end of an Himalayan expedition I am always content to return to Newcastle upon Tyne, to the hills and rocks of Northumberland and my native North Yorkshire, my first climbing experience being on the sandstone outcrops in Scugdale whist still a pupil at Northallerton Grammar School. After moving to Teacher Training College in Newcastle, I started to visit the outcrops of Northumberland and slowly developed a fondness for their unique ambience and these wild and unspoilt regions continue to draw me into them. My original favourite was Crag Lough, the routes there being three times the height of most of the sandstone crags in Northumberland. I have always liked stretching the rope out. In my college days I should have visited the sandstone more often. If only I knew then what I know now ...

Sometimes I would stray into the Northumberland hills and crags, such as Henhole on Cheviot, but for most of my weekends I travelled to the Lakes. I would often visit Causey midweek and evenings and even went to Crag Point near Seaton Sluice several times. My preference has always been for leading and I made the mistake of trying to lead the routes at Seaton Sluice. In these days of nice safe indoor walls such as: the Berghaus Wall, Newcastle; Concordia, Cramlington; and Rock Antics, Newton Aycliffe; climbers have not need to visit this dangerous loose and particularly unpleasant cliff. Ironically, now I am experiencing friable and rotten Seaton Sluice like sandstone in the rarefield air of the Himalaya!

My first position as a teacher took me to Hexham. There I was responsible for teaching rock climbing and would often take beginners to the Wanneys and to Shitlington Crag, thus getting to know the cliffs extremely well. Another favourite sandstone crag, also excellent for beginners, was the Belling now, sadly, partially submerged by the Kielder Water Reservoir. It was in the 1980's when I truly discovered and learned to appreciate Northumberland sandstone. After the rigours of the Himalaya what can be more enjoyable than an afternoon or evening at Bowden Doors, Kyloe, Corby's or Simonside? Followed by a pint of cask ale of course.

Northumberland's highest hill, Cheviot, which looks like an uninteresting whale-back, has its hidden gems. It was always infamous for its often waist deep bog on the summit, although there is a sandstone flagged path over the worst bit of the summit trig point. It was always best to go up Cheviot in winter, when the bog was frozen or covered in snow. In winter, Cheviot transforms from a boring blob into a 'real' mountain with excellent skiing and ice climbing. The Hen Hole and Bizzle streams and waterfalls freeze to give good sport in a wild setting.

On one such winter trip to the Bizzle with a local lad in a cold snap I managed to drive up the College Valley, making for a leisurely stroll to the climbing, as opposed to a long bog trot from Langleeford. Approaching the bottom of the route, two NMC climbers, Karin Magog and Steve Crowe, were already ensconced. Steve was grappling with what looked like the main pitch, a 30 – 40 foot section of Grade III water ice. Steve obviously had not been out on ice for a while and was wobbling a little. He always impresses me on the rock with his skill. Now I was impressed by his tenacity and bravery.

I know it is like when you are rusty – it hurts the head a bit! Steve made it and Karin quickly followed. I led behind Karin; it turned out to be a classic pitch of water ice. It is quite bold though as protection was non-existent in the thin, soft ice and there was little in the way of rock protection. Basically it was a solo. Steve and Karin thought it looked easy above and had had enough, so scrambled off and down.

I felt like an outing and decided to follow the frozen water course. At first it was horizontal and easy for a couple of hundred feet, before a 25 foot wall of ice with a corner to the left. I went straight up the ice which was 'sticky' and an excellent Grade II/III pitch. Another Grade II section led around a corner and into a frozen plunge pool, with a 25 foot vertical pillar of ice. I could hardly believe our luck to get a pitch like this. It was short but sweet, a few vertical moved and it was all over too soon, but we had climbed the "Bizzle Integral".

The Cheviot still would not let us off its flanks easily though and we had to carefully and tentatively traverse and descent avalanche – prone slopes, loaded with windslab. It was just like the real thing. It was the real thing and yet I was back for a pint in Newcastle that night, well satisfied with a memorable and fine winter experience.

Why go to the Himalayas when on can reap the rewards and enjoy the pleasure of the hills of Northumberland? Perhaps it is necessary to go to the greater ranges to understand the splendours of one's own back yard.

Alan Hinkes succeeded in climbing K2 in July 1995.

Recent Developments in Northumberland Climbing 1989 – 94
John Earl

The publication of a new guide book generally stimulates interest and activity in an area, for everyone except those involved in its production, who are usually ready for a change or a rest. After the publication of the 1989 Northumberland guide Bob Smith and I concentrated our efforts outside the County, leaving the field clear for the next generation. Developments since that time have fallen into three categories: routes on the existing major crags; routes on new esoteric crags; bouldering on anything that doesn't move.

Firstly, the major crags in the north of the County continued to attract attention, with Bowden Doors being the scene of early activity by Karl Telfer accompanied by Joe Gillespey and Steve Roberts on Peace at Last, just left of Outward Bound. This was followed by the return of Dave "Cubby" Cuthbertson after a long absence, to climb the oft fancied and occasionally attempted line at the left end of the Merlin wall, to give County Ethics (Never too Old to Rock and Roll) E7, 7a, which utilised a rock 'n' roller for protection, giving the hardest route in the County at the time. Dave Pegg then produced his trilogy of hard routes at Back Bowden in 1991, The Pixie, King Lear and Big Ariel Dynamite, before leaving the area to live in Sheffield.

At Bowden Doors Richard Davies just missed the cut with his ascent of Imagery, which starts up Slab Crack and then goes left. This was followed by Ian Cumming's traverse under the Wave to give Rip the Lip, the following year. In 1991 Hugh Harris attacked the Wave to give Narcosis and Inner Space, both with Joe Webb and Daniel Pattison.

Bob Smith and John Earl continued in The Woods in 1990 with Sex and Brutality and Hostile Environment and Hugh Harris and Joe Webb ventured to the Quarry, Out of the Woods in 1991 to climb The Seventh Day.

The higher crags also attracted attention, mainly from Hugh Harris and friends to provide some excellent routes. At Ravensheugh there were some plums waiting to be picked and Hugh probably got the best of the crop with First Among Equals, which takes the 'weakness' in the wall left of Ravensheugh Crack. July 1989 was a good month for Hugh. He also climbed Lapse of Reason and Paradise Lost on which he was accompanied by Rhian and Joe Webb and on Castaway he joined forces with Tim Gallagher. Also in 1989 Richard Davies with Graham Telfer and Joe Gillespey climbed Agape from out of Trouser Legs.

Great Wanney, in 1990, gave Hugh Harris and Ian Cummings Policy of Truth, up the wall and crack right of Endless Flight, which Hugh followed up in 1991 with his ascent of Crisis Zone, up the steep wall right of Absent Friend at E7, 6c to give one of the hardest routes in the County. Also in 1991 Richard Davies and Andy Wilkinson added Katana, just right of Great Wall and Steve Crowe traversed East Buttress to give Eastern Ecstasy.

Sandy Crag got the Hugh Harris treatment when he climbed Victims of Circumstance with Rhian Webb and Living on Borrowed Time. Joe Webb, who was a relative novice at the time, climbed the arete right of The Slot to give an E6, 6b, Time and Motion.

Howlerhirst, which hadn't had a significant new route since Tommy Smith's Guardian Angel, was the scene of Richard Davies, Neil Brunger and Joe Gillespey's Devil's Soulmate and Dave Pegg and Lewis Grundy's Where Angels Tread. Also, the age old Rothbury Quarry saw its old pegged wall freed by Karl Telfer in 1991.

The second area of activity was the continuous search for the second Kyloe In or Bowden Doors.

The bad news is that no-one has found it yet. The further bad news is that new crags have been discovered and then in some cases, amazingly, developed. Details of some of these are as follows. Boyes Quarry, situated near Corby's, originally climbed on by Steve Blake, was re-discovered and developed by Will Walker and John McRoberts. Dove Hole Crag, a 'bouldering' crag near Goat's Crag, where routes have been cleaned and climbed by Tim Gallagher, Simon Berry and Dave Barrel. Coquet View, an impressive crag adjacent to Ravensheugh, was gardened by Hugh Harris, Jeff Ross, Rhian and Joe Webb, following a tip-off from Bob Smith and myself. Homestead Crag was found on Beaney Moor by George and Chris Ridge. The Mount, just South of Powburn, was discovered by Paul Linfoot and Taff Hughes, following tree felling. Thrum Mill Crag on the River Coquet, just east of Rothbury, which was climbed originally by Gordon Thompson in the 70s was re-discovered by Simon Gee and Lewis Grundy.

The County's number one new crag sniffer, Malcolm Lowerson, has continued where he left off with Howns Gill, developing Eglingham Quarry, Hareshaw Linn, Blawearie and, most recently Curtis Crag which is probably on much better rock than the others.

Leaving the best until last, Whiteheugh Crag was revisited after a long absence by John Earl and Bob Smith and subsequently developed by Steve Crowe and Karin Magog, assisted by Bob Smith and John and Andrew Earl. The best routes of the crag are True Grit, which takes the obvious thin crack and was climbed by Steve Blake at E4, 6b in the 70s, White Lies E4, 6c (something not right here!) which Steve Crowe climbed to its left and Bones Don't Bounce (even when you are 16) E5/6, 6b which Andrew Earl climbed on his second attempt, thinking it was probably a mild Extreme, having fallen, stripped the gear and not bounced on his first attempt.

The third area of development has been the resurgence of bouldering – not the soloing of easy or not so easy routes – but the execution of one or two hard and in some cases desperate moves on small areas of rock, often with the chalk bag scraping the ground. The main ingredients are good rock, good landings, accessibility and a good imagination. The main protagonists in this area have been Alec Burns, Bob Smith, Steve Crowe, Andrew Earl, John Earl and Karin Magog. The best areas to date are Rothley Boulders, Caller Boulders, Ravensheugh Boulders, Shaftoe Boulders, Crag X and Crag A-Z, plus hundreds of sections on the existing crags.

Well, that was more or less the state of play in Northumberland climbing until 1994. Then Malcolm Smith, an exceptional young talent from Dunbar, who had been climbing and training on the North Northumberland crags for some years, completed his boulder problem/stamina trip, Leviathan (Font 8b+) at Kyloe in the Woods.

Steve Roberts then claimed the hardest route in the county with I Bet He Drinks Carling Black Label, weighing in at E8, 6c at Back Bowden Doors, which was followed by Malcolm Smith's ascent of possibly the hardest route in the country, Transcendence, E9, 7a. Subsequently, however, this has been repeated whereas Steve's route still awaits a second ascent.

Northumberland climbing certainly seems to be thriving, with more and more people on the crags. I just hope that the more popular crags can cope with this heavy traffic. The ethics regarding top-roping have slipped a little but I'm sure we can live with this, providing every care is taken to prevent damage to the rock. What the majority of local activists will not tolerate, however, is chipping or the use of sika cement to alter holds. The blank walls are there for this generation and future generations. I, therefore, implore today's climbers not to deprive the next generation of their inheritance, in the pursuit of transient glory.

Access to the Secluded County
Nigel and Heather Jamieson

Northumberland, best regarded for the lonely wind swept moorland, forest and isolated crags rolling northward in a sea of purple and grey, is a unique county. Unique in the sense that even as the twenty first century approaches it still offers seclusion, solitude and remoteness.

Climbing however has in the last ten years or so contributed to a gradual change. It is a burgeoning sport. Many crags now receive dozens of climbers, encouraged by magazine articles extolling the delights of our sandstone crags. The pressure on the environment is growing, three or four of the principal crags being particularly vulnerable. The once remote vastness is slowly being lost.

The County is still feudal in nature. The vast area of Northumberland being owned by a small number of landowners, several tracing their rights of ownership to the dark days of the sword and being born into the right family. The majority of our crags and climbing areas are privately owned and we pursue our sport as uninvited guests. Access arrangements have always been tenuous and reliant upon the goodwill of the landowner.

The increasing popularity of climbing has brought with it problems of access. Owners have understandably been concerned about damage to forest, crops and fences and indeed some damage has occurred. Great efforts have been made to ensure that these problems are kept to a minimum. In the last ten years negotiations by the NMC have helped retain access to a few major climbing areas, notably, Ravensheugh, Sandy Crag, and outcrops within the vast military training area of Otterburn. Notices have been built at all the popular crags advising climbers of their responsibilities. Stiles have been erected, litter regularly removed and even dumped cars have been winched off at Corby's Crag, with the kind assistance of the army.

Despite the efforts of the club, pressure is continually increasing with regard to the access situation. Excessive use at Kyloe, Bowden Doors, and indeed Back Bowden Doors are creating serious erosion problems. This pressure being brought about by sheer numbers of climbers. The increasing popularity of youth group and outdoor centre activities has also added to the pressure, particularly in the north Northumberland area. Access cannot be taken for granted. We are totally forbidden to climb at Shitlington and East Woodburn despite extensive negotiations. Careless use of these crags by youth groups and individual climbers is the cause of the ban.

The problems in the County are well acknowledged by the British Mountaineering Council. Members of the club attend regular meetings of the BMC to discuss and co-ordinate plans to retain and gain access to climbing areas. The club has acted as a leader in the field of access negotiation over a number of years, conducting these negotiations with a wide variety of owners from the military to titled absentee landlords. Despite our success clouds lie over the horizon.

Nationally access problems appear to be more frequent. Climbers must be aware of major problems brought about by new government legislation. Walkers, ramblers and climbers who challenge landowners, now face fines and imprisonment under the Criminal Justice and Public Order Bill. A new offence of aggravated trespass has been created. Trespass is now a criminal offence. Particular problems have arisen recently in North Yorkshire and Lancashire with land owners preventing entry onto vast tracts of grouse moor. These problems will certainly spread north into the County.

Forestry Commission privatisation lies over the horizon. Temporarily held in abeyance by the government, it poses a potential threat to climbers and their rights of access to the wilder areas of Northumberland. In addition a watchful eye on the expansion of the Otterburn ranges in the Cheviot foot hills needs to be maintained. No one person or body should, have the right to deny access to the public to our land and indeed our beautiful County that is our heritage. We have to retain the right to roam freely.

The next fifty years will obviously see new access problems raised. However, the club, ever mindful of its role in Northumberland's climbing activities, will continue to remain vigilant, and will act whenever necessary to retain the rights of all climbers and those who enjoy the County, to climb and walk at will.

The outlook would appear bleak but given the climate's natural inbuilt resistance to authority and the overall appreciation of Northumberland's natural beauty we are convinced that many of the problems that we face will be overcome.

As a final reminder to the reader please remember we are uninvited guests. Follow the access advice in the guide and have a great time on the crag. Take nothing from the crag but photographs and pleasant memories, and leave nothing behind but footprints.

Selected First Ascents List
Compiled by Steve Crowe

This selective first ascents list for Northumberland has been compiled using the following criteria:

1. All the starred routes in the current (1989) guide book;
2. Most of the starred routes in the 1992 supplement;
3. A selection of the routes climbed since 1992;
4. Date and names of first recorded free ascent.

It is the intention of the NMC to include a complete first ascents list in the next climbing guide and it is hoped that readers with missing facts will pass on the information to: Steve Crowe, 9 Maplebeck Close, Sunderland, telephone (0191) 525 2025. Names of first ascentionists, dates and anecdotes will all be appreciated. It is understood that in the early days many of the routes were considered as just training for the Lake District and bigger crags and, therefore, first ascents were not recorded. However, if routes can be associated with a year (even a decade) and a group/team/club (eg: Crag Lough/Wanneys Climbing Club) then we will be able to bring the list up to date.

BACK BOWDEN DOORS

7 August 1991
Big Aerial Dynamite Dave Pegg
An extended boulder problem

31 January 1992
Boulder Lands Julian Lines

Autumn 1990
County Ethics/Never Too Old to Rock and Roll
Dave Cuthbertson
Still the hardest "safe" route in Northumberland?

1977
Duke of York John Earl and Bob Hutchinson
Not quite all the way to the top and back again.

1979
Dwarfs Nightmare Tommy Smith and Bob Smith
Tom, 6'1", weighed in at 10 stone for this one move wonder!

1 August 1978
Hard Reign Bob Hutchinson and John Earl

Hazelrigg Wall

Holly Bush Crack

Holly Tree Corner

20 June 1994
I Bet He Drinks Carling Black Label
Stephen Roberts
Probably the best climb in the world! Unrepeated.

26 June 1991
King Lear Dave Pegg
Powerful but protectable

26 June 1994
Leap of Faith Malcolm Smith
A hard direct start to Lost Cause

1979
Lost Cause Tommy Smith and Bob Smith
Now available on video – contact: A Birtwistle

1 September 1987
Macbeth Bob Smith and John Earl
A bold and technical route

1976
Magic Flute Malcolm Rowe and Nev Hannaby

14 August 1981
Merlin Bob Smith and John Earl
The first breach of this impressive north wall

1987
Mordreth Bob Smith

1986
Morgan Bob Smith and Tommy Smith

28 November 1987
On the Rocks Bob Smith
Bob, discovering that Tom had top-roped the line got in first

18 May 1977
On the Verge John Earl and Bob Hutchinson
It may be possible to jump on to the ledge on the right

Original Route

1 August 1979
Outward Bound Paul Stewart and John Earl
Aptly named

1987
Peak Technique Tony Coutts
Claimed in his slippers, importing Derbyshire ethics

27 June 1985
Right of Reply Bob Smith
Essentially a hard and sustained extension of The Tube

1973
Roof Route Hugh Banner

1981
Shackletack John Earl, Bob Smith and Ian Kyle
Which witches pet?

c1968
Sorcerer's Apprentice Ken Wood

Straight Crack

1965
The Arches Rodney Wilson
A good effort for 1965

1975
The Broomstick John Earl and Bob Hutchinson

1 March 1975
The Enchanter Bob Hutchinson and John Earl
Virtually a solo and graded as such

31 May 1991
The Pixies Dave Pegg

1968
The Sorcerer Allan Austin and Dave Roberts
The fist discovery of the "magic" of Back Bowden

1978
The Spell Jeff Lamb and Steve Blake
A stranger in the county

1978
The Tube Bob Hutchinson and John Earl
A possible escape from Uncouth Youth

The Vole Bob Hutchinson
Worth getting out of your hole for

1978
The Wand John Earl and Bob Hutchinson

1974
The Witch Malcolm Rowe and Nev Hannaby
The first route on the central wall

17 June 1978
The Wizard Bob Smith

26 June 1994
Transcendence Malcolm Smith
A spectacular and popular line!

27 June 1985
Uncouth Youth Bob Smith and John Earl
A possible escape route from Right of Reply!

Wall and Crack

When the Wind Blows
Karl Telfer and Graham Telfer

BERRYHILL

Border Ballad

1982
Death or Glory Bob Smith

1982
Do or Die Bob Smith

Eastern Arete

Reiver's Way

The Flutings

Marcher Lord Ken MacDonald
Climbed in the early 1970s

THE BIZZLE

Bizzle Burn
The county's best winter route

BOWDEN DOORS

February 1974
Abanana Bob Hutchinson and John Earl

Banana Wall
22 October 1978

Barbarian Bob Smith
A hard solo. Very bold. No-one could come near to Bob's tenacity.

Black and Tan

Bloody Crack

Bloody Nose

24 July 1978
Boomer John Earl and Bob Hutchinson

1967
Canada Crack Eric Rayson
His last notable climb before leaving to live in Canada

Castle Crack

1988
Death Knell Mark Liptrot

1977
Don't Let Go Steve Blake

Exhibition Crack Tommy Smith and Bob Smith
Named after their other favourite pastime!

10 July 1980
First Century Bob Smith, John Earl and Ian Kyle

First Leaning Groove Malcolm Rowe

June 1978
Goose Step Bob Hutchinson and John Earl

Grovel Groove

Guard's Exit

1972
Hanging Crack Hugh Banner
Immediately after Allan Austin backed off it

2 September 1979
High Tide Bob Smith

27 September 1980
His Eminence Bob Smith

22 May 1991
Inner Space
Hugh Harris, Joe Webb and Daniel Pattison

Introductory Staircase

10 July 1980
Kaiser Bill Bob Smith

Klondyke Wall Steve Blake

5 May 1978
Leo Bob Smith

Long Crack

Lorraine Malcolm Rowe
First known on sight lead in 1968

1969
Main Wall Malcolm Rowe

Main Wall Eliminate Paul Stewart

Outer Limits Karl Telfer

Pitcher Wall

Poseidon Adventure Steve Blake
The first route to break through the wave

16 May 1984
Poverty Bob Smith
Poorly endowed with holds

Retreat Alan Austin
After backing off what would have been the FA of Hanging Crack

10 September 1990
Rip the Lip Ian Cummings
Surfing

10 July 1979
Rising Damp Bob Smith
The first 6b on Bowden Doors

1988
Rough Passage Bob Smith and John Earl

Russet Groove
Possibly the most impressive climb of its grade in the country

Scoop 1

Scoop 2

Scorpion
Aptly named

Second Leaning Groove

Slab Crack

9 June 1979
Street Runner Bob Smith

1972/73
Stretcher Wall John Earl and Bob Hutchinson
If you can't make the reach you might need one!

Sue

Temptation John Welford

29 October 1983
The Bends Bob Smith
On sight solo. Could lead to a bad head!

1978
The Gauleiter John Earl and Bob Hutchinson
The first ascentionist's nick name

The Manta Jeff Lamb
Turned out to be a wolf in sheep's clothing

1971/72
The Overhanging Crack
John Earl and Bob Hutchinson
First climbed with a rest on a chockstone by John Hiron

31 May 1978
The Rajah Bob Smith
The first "unrecognised" 6b on Bowden

November 1972
The Runnel John Earl

The Scoop

May 1975
The Sting Bob Hutchinson and John Earl
Also claimed by R Redford and P Newman!

1972
The Trial Bob Hutchinson
BH first significant route and the hardest on the crag then

The Viper

July 1978
The Wave Bob Hutchinson

Tiger's Wall
Don't feed your friends to this tiger

1977
Transformer Steve Blake
Don't transform the route description, rarely all climbed

Triple Cracks

Woolman's Wall Alan Austin
Named after Austin's chosen profession

BROOMLEE LOUGH CRAG

Consolation Tommy Smith

25 July 1988
The Throwback John Earl

CALLERHUES

Boulevard Steve Blake

Callerhues' Chimney
John Earl and Bob Hutchinson
In the dim and distant past!

Callerhues' Crack Everyone!

1988
Chouca Bob Smith

15 April 1978
Copper's Nark

1979
Crouching the Mahogany Bob Smith

5 March 1978
Cut and Dried

Dick

Dolcis Arete Tommy Smith
If the boot fits, wear it. Dolcis is the name of an old shoe shop.

15 April 1978
Footpath Bob Smith

28 May 1978
Green Fluff Bob Smith
Named because of the green fluff left by a fibre pile jacket

Hanging Crack Bob Smith

Harry

22 September 1979
Horse Play Bob Smith

23 April 1979
Ned Kelly Bob Smith
Tin hat recommended

Quarrel Arete Bob Smith
(Or brothers in arms?)

Raindrops Tommy Smith

Rice Krispies Tommy Smith

10 July 1985
Second Born Bob Smith
Bob's a dad again!

Sheer Temptation

2 April 1978
Task Master Bob Smith
Tommy might have thought he was …

28 May 1978
The Hyena Bob Smith

21 May 1978
The Lurcher Bob Smith

21 May 1978
The Mongrel Bob Smith

1988
The Story Teller Bob Smith

The Thoroughbred Tommy Smith

Tom

Tom's Peeping Bob Smith

1984
Toshiba Receiver Allan Moist and Dave Carr

9 April 1978
Weeping Fingers Bob Smith

Flake Wall

COE CRAG

Black Walter Chimney

1984
Cave Wall
Hugh Harris, John Wallace and Graham Telfer

1968
Coe Crag Corner Allan Austin and Dave Roberts

1968
Hippopotamus Allan Austin and Dave Roberts

1968
Honeycomb Wall Allan Austin and Dave Roberts

1971
Neb Crack Hugh Banner

1984
Orion Roof
Hugh Harris, John Wallace and Graham Telfer
With a pre-placed friend in the roof

1984
Rampart Wall
Hugh Harris, John Wallace and Graham Telfer

1968
Raven's Buttress Dave Roberts and Allan Austin

1971
Rough Castles Crack
Dave Roberts and Ernie Goodyear

Twin Cracks

CORBY'S CRAG

1979
Ash Wednesday Bob Smith and Tommy Smith

1971
Audacity Ken MacDonald and John Earl

1970
Black Wall Ken MacDonald and John Earl

1970
Bloody Sunday
Ken MacDonald, John Earl and Ian Cranston

Bluebird Steve Blake
It was rated as hard as Australia Crack at the time – it is!

Bogeyman Ken MacDonald and John Earl

September 1973
Corbeau Bob Hutchinson
Named after a Jackdaw

September 1973
Friday's Child John Earl and Bob Hutchinson

1974
Gibbon's Gambol Bob Hutchinson

Hole-in-One
John Earl, Bob Hutchinson and Ian Cranston

Ken's Caper Ken MacDonald

LP Ken MacDonald, John Earl and Ian Cranston

Man Friday Ken MacDonald

Misrepresentation Ken MacDonald

1977
Ranadon Martin Doyle and Karl Telfer

Sunshine Superman Ken MacDonald and John Earl
But did they free it?

1970
Temptation Ken MacDonald, John Earl and Ian Cranston

1977
Tenacity Jeff Lamb

The Plonka Ken MacDonald

August 1977
Tiger Feet Steve Blake

CRAG LOUGH

Ash Tree Wall

Back Alley

Block Chimney

Block Chimney Super Direct

Bracket

Centurion's Crack Tony Moulam with T P Snell, Gosman and other locals

Chariot Race Jeff Lamb

Crescent Cracks Albert Rosher with Frank Carroll, Don Laws and Geoff Oliver

Crystal

Dexterity

Evasion Groove

Grad's Groove Brian Cooke and Bob Conn

Great Chimney Marcus Beresford Heywood
Recorded in the 1912 Climbers' Club Journal

Hadrian's Recess

Hadrian's Rib

Hadrian's Buttress

Helix Tony Moulam with T P Snell, Gosman and other locals

Hoozit's Crack Tony Moulam with T P Snell, Gosman and other locals
Moulam was Hoozit

Impossible Wall Jeff Lamb

Jezebel

Left Organ Pipe Tony Moulam with T P Snell, Gosman and other locals

Main Wall Marcus Beresford Heywood
*Recorded in the 1912 Climbers' Club Journal.
Also attributed to Basil Butcher and Keith Gregory, 1940s*

Main Wall Route 2

Main Wall Route 2, Direct Finish

Neglect Nev Hannaby

Pinnacle Face

Raven's Tower

Right Organ Pipe Tony Moulam with T P Snell, Gosman and other locals

Route 1 (Impossible Buttress)
Tony Moulam and Alf Mullan
Belayed with homemade pegs!

Route 3 (Impossible Wall) Albert Rosher with Frank Carroll, Don Laws and Geoff Oliver

Sciatica Albert Rosher with Frank Carroll, Don Laws and Geoff Oliver

Sinister Corner

4 June 1978
Spot the Dog The Smiths

Spuggies Gulley

5 May 1980
Stephenson's Rocket Bob Smith and Tommy Smith

Tarzan

Tarzan's Mate

3 September 1991
The Stone Warrior Hugh Harris and Rhian Webb

1976
Whinstone Churchill
Bob Hutchinson and John Earl

Whinstone Churchill Direct Bill Wayman

Why Not Albert Rosher with Frank Carroll, Don Laws and Geoff Oliver

Why Not Direct

4 June 1978
Wooden Tops Bob Smith and Tommy Smith

Y Climb Albert Rosher with Frank Carroll, Don Laws and Geoff Oliver
Why not!

CULLERNOSE POINT

Frank's Rib Malcolm Rowe
Malcolm climbed it because Frank couldn't

1978
Johnathan Livingstone Seagull
Bob Hutchinson and John Earl

1978
Nerve Wrack Point Bob Hutchinson and John Earl

Ochre Wall Alan Austin
First recorded ascent during the late 1960s

Original Route possibly Peter Biven and Bob Ower
Many of the early ascents were by this team during 1954/55

1976
The Deep Bob Hutchinson and John Earl

Zero G Malcolm Rowe
An excellent free route, on this unpopular crag

18 September 1994
Shot in the Dark Malcolm Lowerson
The best line of the many climbed by Malcolm here

DRAKE STONE

Plymouth Hoe Bob Hutchinson and John Earl

7 August 1983
Powder Monkey Bob Smith

Rhumba Dave Adams

Sir Francis Bob Hutchinson

The Golden Hind Bob Hutchinson and John Earl

The Pelican

EAST WOODBURN

Autobahn Paul Linfoot and Andy Winter

Death Wish Paul Linfoot and Andy Winter

1960s
Green Slab Gordon Thompson

1960s
Green Wall Gordon Thompson

Ridsdale Wall

1980s
The Arbitrator
Karl Telfer, Graham Telfer and Joe Gilespy

Trans Europe Express
Paul Linfoot and Andy Winter

Woodburn Wall Gordon Thompson

GOAT'S CRAG

Belford Chip Shop Andy Moss

1972
Bull Wall John Earl, Bob Hutchinson, Dennis Lee and Ian Cranston

5 January 1980
Convoy Bob Smith, Paul Stewart and John Earl

Double Trouble

Flyover Graham Telfer, Karl Telfer and Joe Gilhespy

1972
Guano Groove Bob Hutchinson, John Earl, Dennis Lee and Ian Cranston

1 July 1981
Hard Shoulder Bob Smith

1987
Imminent Break Crisis
Andy Moss and Colin Murley
Second ascent available on video – contact: A Birtwistle

Juggernaut Paul Stewart, Bob Smith and John Earl

Kangaroo Court

5 January 1980
Lost Arete Bob Smith

October 1977
Overdrive Bob Hutchinson
You need one for this route, go for it

1988
Ruth Route
Karl Telfer, Graham Telfer and Joe Gilespy

14 January 1973
The Dagger John Earl and Bob Hutchinson

1972
Triangular Slab Bob Hutchinson, John Earl, Dennis Lee and Ian Cranston

Twin Cam Bob Smith, Paul Stewart and John Earl

Undercarriage

Underpass Steve Blake
If you fail on Overdrive don't go for this

1972
Wool Ball Bob Hutchinson, John Earl, Dennis Lee and Ian Cranston

GOAT'S BUTTRESS

20 October 1991
The Dungeon Tim Gallagher

20 October 1991
The Hesitant Roofer
Tommy Smith and Tim Gallagher

GREAT DOUR CRAG

Culloden John Earl and Bob Hutchinson

The Bagpipes

GREAT WANNEY

'B' Crack

24 July 1981
Absent Friend Bob Smith and John Earl
In remembrance of Bob Hutchinson

1978
Blue Arete Bob Smith and Tommy Smith

Boundary Corner
Probably a very early ascent

1978
Broken Wing Bob Hutchinson and John Earl

California Crack Hugh Banner
May have been climbed previously by others

Central Gully
Geoffrey Winthrop Young certainly climbed this route in 1902

East Buttress Direct
Bob Hutchinson and John Earl

14 August 1991
Eastern Ecstacy Steve Crowe
An upsidedown hands off rest can be taken!

Eastern Traverse

Foxes Hole
Geoffrey Winthrop Young certainly climbed this route in 1902

Great Chimney
Geoffrey Winthrop Young certainly climbed this route in 1902

1971
Great Wall Hugh Banner and Mick Foggin
Hugh had led every route on Cloggy except for Great Wall!

28 July 1979
Great Wall Direct John Syrett

Hawk Slab

5 September 1976
Idiot Wind Bob Hutchinson

Idiot's Delight Hugh Banner

Jacob's Ladder

1978
Last Retreat Bob Smith and Tommy Smith

Lees Leap Hugh Banner

Main Wall

30 April 1977
Northumberland Wall
Bob Hutchinson and John Earl
One of the best for its grade and protection in the country

Nosey Parker Bob Hutchinson and John Earl
Named after Steve Blake's curiosity about what Bob was up to

Obverse Direct

1980
Osiris John Earl and Paul Stewart

Patchett's Plunge Hugh Banner and Mike Foggin
Named after Jim Patchett who had a nasty fall on an early attempt

Pharaoh's Face Hugh Banner and David Ladkin
Originally done in two pitches with a hanging stance and graded VS

April 1980
Pitfall Paul Stewart and John Earl

10 June 1991
Policy of Truth Hugh Harris and Ian Cummings

Rake's Crack Hugh Banner and David Ladkin
Nice finger jamming at the top. Hughies speciality

Raven's Nest
Geoffrey Winthrop Young certainly climbed this route in 1902

Spider Crack Hugh Banner

1986
Stairway to Heaven John Wallace

1964
The Brute Geoff Oliver

18 May 1991
The Crisis Zone Hugh Harris

14 June 1978
The Last Retreat Bob Smith
Originally named Fast Retreat

16 April 1980
Thin Ice Bob Smith and Martin Doyle

3 July 1980
Thunder Thighs Bob Smith and John Earl

Two Tear Crack Jim Patchett
Possibly with aid, Hugh Banner climbed it free in the early 70s

West Chimney
Geoffrey Winthrop Young certainly climbed this route in 1902

Willing to Sin

HECKLEY

Liquorice Torpedo Steve Blake and Kirton
Early use of friends in the county

The Birch Steve Blake

THE HENHOLE CRAGS

Back Adams Corner
Basil Butcher and Keith Gregory

Cannon Hole Direct
Basil Butcher and Keith Gregory
Tarver and Glover described how to reach the Cannon Hole in 1899

College Grooves
Phillip McGill and Harry Warmington
One of the best severes in the county

Conception Corner

Fingery Jim Malcolm Lowerson and Jim Patchett
One of many new routes by this team at Henhole

25 June 1983
Funeral Pyre Steve Crowe
This first ascent was only claimed after the insistence of N Hannaby. Ta Nev.

Misconception

Long John Phillip McGill and Harry Warmington

Platform and Chimney

Steerpike Jim Patchett

The Brute Jim Patchett

The Egg

Tombstone Phillip McGill and Harry Warmington

1987
Zeus the Mighty Bull
Calum Henderson and Lee Clegg

Zig-Zag Basil Butcher and Keith Gregory

HOWLERHIRST

10 September 1989
Devil's Soul Mate
Richard Davies, Neil Brunger and Joe Gilhespy
Bold

19 October 1991
Where Angels Fear to Tread
Dave Pegg and Lewis Grundy

1979
Guardian Angel Tommy Smith
Climbed in EB's, this route was well ahead of its time

Howlerhirst Chimney possibly Gordon Thompson
Hugh Banner climbed it circa 1971

THE JACK ROCK

August 1974
Ancient Briton Bob Hutchinson and John Earl

11 July 1979
Barracuda Roof Tommy Smith and Bob Smith
Never fail when Bob Smith is holding your rope or you get "Shall I have a go?"

Breakout Kev Howett and Andy Nelson

1959/1960s
Devil's Wedge probably Malcolm Lowerson

1959/1960s
Dry Fly Corner probably Malcolm Lowerson

Greenwell's Glory John Earl and Bob Hutchinson

Hanging Tree

High Board Malcolm Lowerson

31 December 1988
Jack of All Trades Dave Turnbull

Pause and Ponder probably Malcolm Lowerson

Salmon Leap probably Malcolm Lowerson

The Angler John Earl and Bob Hutchinson

March 1973
The Butcher Bob Hutchinson and John Earl

1959/1960s
Wet Fly Malcolm Lowerson
Malcolm was the Wet Fly after an early attempt!

KYLOE CRAG

before October 1977
Australia Crack Bob Hutchinson
The first 6b in the county

18 October 1980
Baptism Bob Smith

Birdlime Crack

Chris's Arete Chris Fuller

Christmas Tree Arete

Cloister Wall

1970
Coldstream Corner
Allan Austin and Dave Roberts
Climbed after camping on Penitants Walk in Coldstream

circa 1950
Deception Crack
Eric Clark, Gil Lewis and Basil Butcher

Deception Wall

1957
Devil's Edge
Geoff Oliver, Derek Walton and Nev Hannaby

Elder Brother Tommy Smith

29 June 1980
First Born Bob Smith
Overgraded at English 7a! Bob Smith becomes a father

Flake Crack

1 November 1975
Gargarin's Groove John Earl and Bob Hutchinson

Hot Spring Bob Smith and John Earl

Litany

Lost Property Tommy Smith and Bob Smith

1978
Original Sin Steve Blake and Bob Smith
First use of chalk on a new route in the county by a local

Parity David Ladkin and Hugh Banner

Paternoster John Earl and Bob Smith

Penitent's Walk Allan Austin and Dave Roberts
After a night camped on Penitent's Walk near Coldstream

Prime Time Steve Blake
Solo. Blake showing how good he was at that time

Slab and Groove

Slab and Wall

Space Walk Bob Hutchinson and John Earl

St Ivel

1957
Tacitation Nev Hannaby

The Elevator David Ladkin
Who pulled the block off?

The Pincer John Earl and Bob Hutchinson

1 November 1980
The Sabbath
Bob Smith, Steve Blake and Paul Stewart

3 October 1991
The Seventh Day Hugh Harris and Joe Webb

circa 1950
Trinity Eric Clark, Gil Lewis and Basil Butcher

10 March 1979
Wasted Time Bob Smith
A misnomer if ever there was one

Wilfred Prickles John Earl
The gorse bush has long since gone

KYLOE IN THE WOOD

October 1979
Autowind Paul Stewart

Bad Company Paul Stewart

circa 1976
Badfinger Bob Hutchinson and John Earl

Bobby Dazzler Bob Hutchinson

January 1969
Crack of Gloom Allan Austin and Dave Roberts

Crucifixion Hugh Banner

Dingley Dell Bob Hutchinson

Green Man Bob Smith
High cost in time and dirt (clean route!)

1986
High Society Tim Gallagher and Tommy Smith
Tim was white on the last move – he had good right to be

June 1978
High T Bob Hutchinson and John Earl
A Hugh Banner attempt in the early 70s stopped at the "T"

1978/79
Hitchhikers Guide to the Galaxy Steve Blake
The first 6c in the county by using two odd boots

9 February 1985
Jocks and Geordies Dave Cuthbertson,
Murray Hamilton and Bob Smith, John Earl, Ian Kyle
Geordies on top!

11 June 1978
Penny Whistle Bob Smith

Piano

Piccolo

Pink Gin Bill Wayman and Paul Stewart
First ascent may have been Dave Cuthbertson

Primitive Crack

Red Rum Bob Hutchinson and John Earl

Stirring Up Trouble Steve Blake

Swan Wall Direct Steve Blake

The Crucifix Hugh Banner

The Elf

The Elf Direct Steve Blake

The Entertainer Bob Hutchinson and John Earl

The Flutings Direct

The Gauntlet Rod Valentine
Possibly the hardest route in the woods at that time

The Harp

The Missing Link
Hugh Banner, David Ladkin and Mick Foggin
Soon to become the missing route – more traffic please

The Pearler John Earl

Thin Hand Special Hugh Banner
Hugh demonstrated a no hands rest by using knee jam halfway up

1979
Trouble Shooter Paul Stewart
Chicken heads disappearance made it harder

20 December 1986
Upper Crust Bob Smith

Verticality

Woodlark

1966
Zed Climb Frank Montgomery
Kyloe in the Woods was on the "secret list" at that time

LINSHIELS ONE

Commando Crack

2 July 1978
The Mercenary Bob Smith and Tommy Smith
Straightened by Bob Smith, 9 June 1982

1973
The Mirage Bob Hutchinson and John Earl

1973
The Phantom Bob Hutchinson and John Earl

MAIDEN CHAMBERS

Barnstormer

PADDA CRAG

22 May 1988
Almighty Voice Colin Murley
On sight solo. Anyone who knows Colin will appreciate the name

Hiawatha

Oregon Trail

1973
Padda Wall
John Earl, Bob Hutchinson and Tim Edmundson

1973
Sike Wall
John Earl, Bob Hutchinson and Tim Edmundson

PEEL CRAG

Ace of Spades Albert Rosher

Albert's Wall

Blasphemy Wall

Captain

Certificate X Albert Rosher
Hard in its day

1958
Green Line Nev Hannaby
Another test piece in its day

Grooves Albert Rosher

Jester

Locomotion Tommy Smith (Free)
Claimed by Jeff Lamb in Crags Magazine. So Tom and Bob sent info

Overhanging Crack Albert Rosher

Parental Guidance

Ritual Bill Wayman and Gordon Landers

Rock Island Line Albert Rosher
Hard in its day

circa 1912
Sunset possibly M B Heywood
Perhaps the best route of its grade in the country

Sunset Direct

Swing Up

24 June 1979
The Intruder Bob Smith and Tommy Smith

Tiger's Overhang

Trilogy

Ulysses

RATCHEUGH CRAG

1954/55
Adam's Folly probably P Biven
Later redeveloped by Ken Smith and the Wanneys CC

1954/55
Delicado probably P Biven
Later redeveloped by Ken Smith and the Wanneys CC

1954/55
Flippertygibbert probably P Biven
Later redeveloped by Ken Smith and the Wanneys CC

1954/55
Muscle Man probably P Biven
Later redeveloped by Ken Smith and the Wanneys CC

1954/55
Narrow Buttress Direct probably P Biven
Later redeveloped by Ken Smith and the Wanneys CC

1954/55
Senapod Corner probably P Biven
Later redeveloped by Ken Smith and the Wanneys CC

RAVEN'S CRAG

Close Encounters Steve Blake

Bottomless Crack (AKA front of Bowden)

Orang Utang (AKA front of Bowden)

Strain in A Vein (AKA front of Bowden)

RAVENSHEUGH

Baluster Crack Allan Austin and Dave Roberts
Named after the vertical fluting

2 July 1979
Billy Biscuit Bob Smith

2 June 1985
Bonneville Bob Smith
... and boy is it fast!

Buckskin Bob Smith
One of Bob's "six in a day"

7 September 1975
Candle in the Wind Bob Hutchinson and John Earl
Years previous Malcolm Rowe got to the last move on-sight!

23 June 1989
Castaway Tim Gallagher and Hugh Harris
Stolen while his best pal (Tommy Smith) was away fishing!

Cat's Whiskers

Childhood's End
Bob Hutchinson
Just before Bob Hutchinson's 30th birthday

Crescent Wall

Easter Grooves

11 June 1989
First Among Equals Hugh Harris
One of Hugh's finest new routes

Futility

10 September 1975
Gates of Eden John Earl and Bob Hutchinson

1970s
Grease Steve Blake
The start of some hard classics, with Concordia training

Half Minute Crack Allan Austin and Dave Roberts
Austin bet that he could climb it in 30 seconds and then did so!

1976
Honeymoon Crack Bob Hutchinson and John Earl
Originally climbed with combined tactics by Geoff Jackson

2 June 1989
Lapse of Reason Hugh Harris
FA was an on-sight solo

Little Leaner

Moccasin Slab Bob Smith
Another of "six in a day" fingers strength courtesy of Concordia

1978
Octopus John Earl and Bob Hutchinson

Old Man River
Paul Stewart and Steve Blake (alt)
Alternate leads. Second ascent solo – Bob Smith

One Boot Crack

5 June 1991
Paradise Lost
Hugh Harris, Rhian Webb and Joe Webb

Pendulum Allan Austin and Dave Roberts
Dave Roberts was the pendulum after falling off the first move!

1 June 1977
Pink Lane Bob Hutchinson

23 July 1977
Plumbline John Earl and Bob Hutchinson

Pussyfoot

1974
Rampart Crack John Earl and Bob Hutchinson

Ravensheugh Crack
Dave Roberts and Hugh Banner (Alt leads or was it Nev H or Geoff O?)
Hugh persuaded Dave to lead to the small ledge. Hugh led the jams!

Redskin Bob Smith
Six in a day!

1984
Rock and Roll Star Bob Smith

Smarty Pants

Soil Stack Crack

St Cuthbert's Crack

The Crescent

27 May 1979
The Judas Hole Bob Smith and Tommy Smith

1978
The Plumber Bob Hutchinson

1974
The Sandrider Bob Hutchinson and John Earl

The Trouser Legs Hugh Banner and David Ladkin
The previous week Hughie took a fall from the crux

1 July 1987
Trial Separation Bob Smith
Solo

5 September 1979
Wide Eyed and Legless Bob Smith and Steve Blake
Bob was, most of the time in those days

Wild West Show Hugh Banner

ROTHLEY CRAG

Dog Burner Karl Telfer, Graham Telfer and D Mould

28 May 1981
Master Blaster Martin Doyle

3 October 1984
Muscular Eruption Bob Smith and John Earl

Rothley Crack First climbed by Jack Longland
The style of this ascent is unsure

The Taste of Someone Else Hugh Harris BMC

SANDY CRAG

circa 1974
Angel Fingers
John Earl, Bob Hutchinson and Ian Cranston

1978
Basil Brush Steve Blake

25 May 1980
Classroom Worm Bob Smith and Tommy Smith

1985
Corporal Punishment John Earl and Bob Smith

Fang Crack

1977
Goldfinger Bob Hutchinson and John Earl

1980
Greenford Road Tommy Smith and Bob Smith
Tommy's address at that time

15 May 1985
Leonardo Bob Smith and John Earl
Another masterpiece

1 August 1990
Living on Borrowed Time Hugh Harris
Hugh survived to tell the tale

1979
Pall Arete Bob Smith

1950s
Question Mark Crack Possibly The College Club

Raven's Nest Crack

22 May 1976
Salvation Bob Hutchinson and John Earl

circa 1974
Sandy Crack John Earl and Bob Hutchinson
A great effort in 1970s gear and boots

25 May 1980
The Anvil Bob Smith and Tommy Smith

22 April 1979
The Jaws Bob Smith and Tommy Smith

1950s
The Vertical Vice Possibly The College Club

1 September 1991
Time and Motion Joe Webb
Joe had only led E4 before this on sight solo first ascent

24 June 1990
Victim of Circumstance
Hugh Harris and Rhian Webb

26 April 1978
Vincent Bob Hutchinson and John Earl

SELBY'S COVE

29 December 1977
Bowline Bob Hutchinson and John Earl

Diagonal

Fosbury's Crack Direct Finish
Peter Kirton with Andy Moss
Recorded as A Non, A Moss

1978
Holly Tree Corner Tommy Smith and Bob Smith
A time of great competition to climb and free routes

pre 1950
Holly Tree Wall

Low Level Girdle

pre 1950
Overhanging Chimney

1964
Overhanging Groove
Eric Rayson, David Moy and Frank Montgomery

pre 1950
The Corner

1976
The Roaring Twenties John Earl
The day before his 30th birthday

pre 1950
The Traverse

SIMONSIDE NORTH FACE

19 September 1991
The Outsider Joe Webb and Hugh Harris

'A' Buttress Right Hand

'B' Buttress Chimney

'D' Buttress Crack

Aeolian Wall Bob Hutchinson and John Earl

Bee Bumble

Cairn Slab

Cairn Wall

1988
Clever Dick Andy Moss and Mark Goodings

6 September 1980
Command Performance Bob Smith
Bob showing that he was in a class of his own in 1980

6 September 1980
Cut Throat Bob Smith and John Earl

1959
Delicatessen Malcolm Lowerson

1978
Dirty Thor't Martin Doyle

Flake Corner

Giant's Stair John Earl

March 1979
Gillette Karl Telfer

Gimme Wings Karl Telfer

Golden Days Karl Telfer

Great Chimney

Innominate Crack

Kyley's Route Ian Kyle

September 1972
Les Perchass
George Micheson, John Earl and Ian Cranston

Lightning Wall John Earl and Bob Hutchinson

Long Layback Crack

Loophole Crack

Master Plaster Graham Telfer

September 1972
Nee Perchass John Earl and Ian Cranston

On the Brink Bob Smith

1978
Over the Edge Jeff Lamb
Over from the Lakes to steal another gem

Quartz Buttress Hugh Banner and David Ladkin
Led on sight by Hugh

Regular Nightmare Bob Smith

Sagittarius Geoff Jackson
Climbed while working on the 1971 guidebook

Smart Alec Andy Moss and Mark Goodings

Swastika Chimney

Swastika Crack

The Quiver Geoff Jackson
Climbed while working on the 1971 guidebook

1979
The Stoic Bob Hutchinson

Thunder Crack
Hugh Banner, David Ladkin and M Foggon
Hugh climbed this again in October 1972 with John Earl and Bob Hutchinson

Top Gun Mark Goodings and Andy Moss

Vibram Wall Possibly Eric Rayson
Originally a peg route

Wellington Crack Andy Moss

Wicked Child Mark Goodings and Andy Moss

circa 1970s
Wise Crack Bob Hutchinson

SOUTH YARDHOPE CRAG

Bran Flakes John Earl and Bob Hutchinson

23 July 1980
Comfortably Numb Paul Stewart and Bob Smith

31 August 1980
Footloose and Flying Free
Bob Smith and Tommy Smith

June 1975
Godzilla Bob Hutchinson and John Earl

Kong Bob Smith and Tommy Smith

Original Route Ken MacDonald

Popcorn Surprise Bob Hutchinson and John Earl
Ask John for the full story

20 June 1984
Priapismic Failure Bob Smith and Andy Moss

August 1980
Quiet County Paul Stewart and John Earl

The Arete Bob Hutchinson

The Camel's Back John Earl and Bob Hutchinson

27 May 1981
The On Sight Gobbler
Bob Smith and Tommy Smith
Named after a nice girl!

The Reaper John Earl

The Splits Bob Hutchinson and John Earl

Yard of Hope John Earl

THRUNTON CRAG

Lord of the Flies Bob Hutchinson
The original Lord of the Flies!

1968
Thrunton Front Malcolm Rowe

WHITEHEUGH CRAG

28 July 1993
Bones Don't Bounce Andrew Earl
He took a spectacular fall on an early attempt and didn't bounce

8 May 1994
White Lies Steve Crowe
Led with pre-placed pro. Success came after about 50 falls!

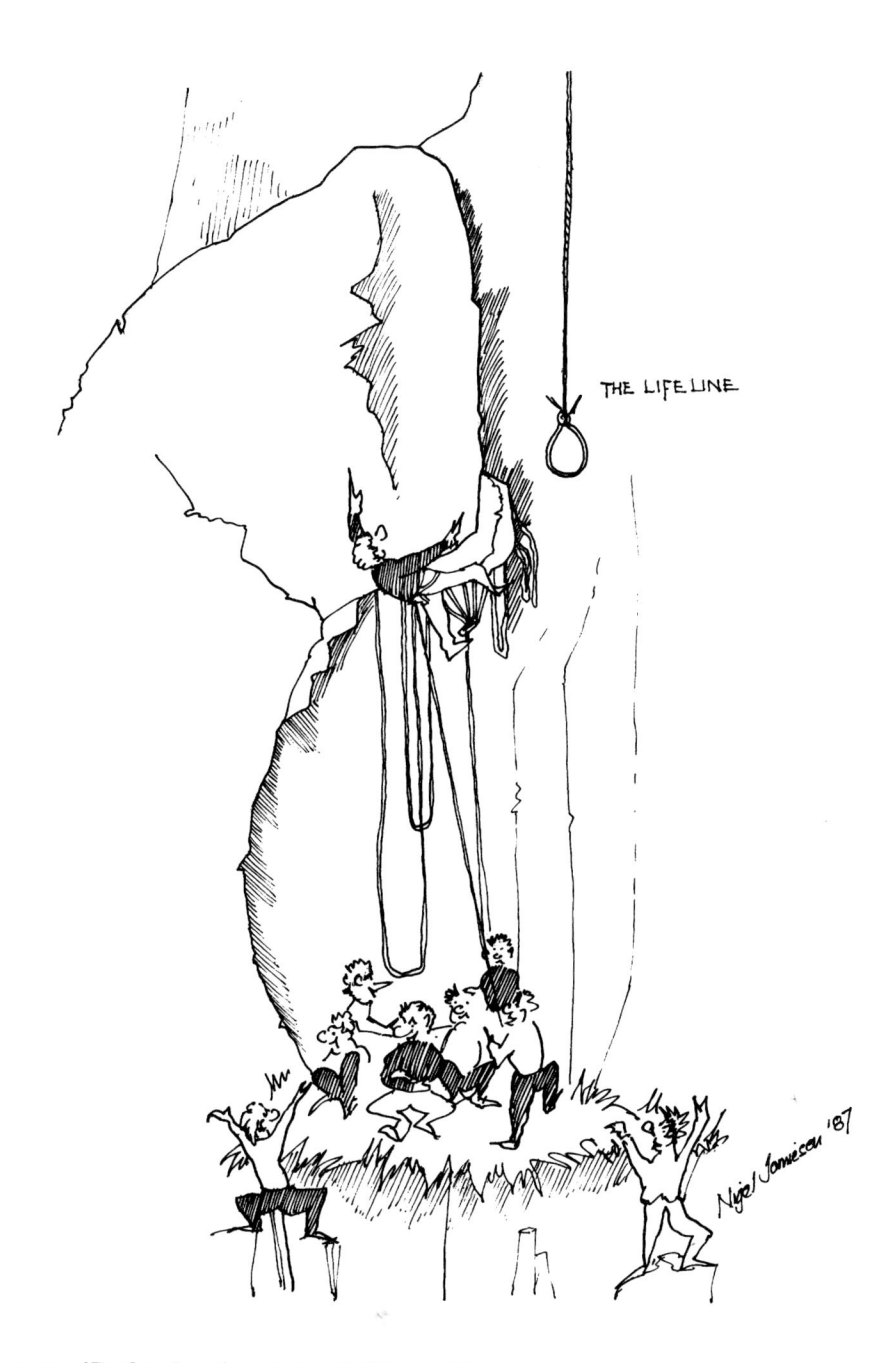

In memory of The Great Flake, Central Buttress, Scafell Crag and Tristram Spence.

To contact the **Northumbrian Mountaineering Club** please write to:

Karin Magog
9 Maplebeck Close
Moorside
Sunderland
SR3 2QU

or telephone: (0191) 520 2520